My good friend, Dr. Bill Henard,
Bones Live? A Practical Guide to C
talization of churches is overwhel.
in this process. Use this as a key resource to help you do so. I surely will.

Johnny M. Hunt, senior pastor,
First Baptist Church, Woodstock, Georgia

Numerous reports indicate that local churches in North America are struggling. With around three-fourths of churches on a growth plateau or in decline, pastors and other church leaders are looking for help in how to revitalize their congregations. *Can These Bones Live?* by Bill Henard is a marvelous resource. Solidly biblical and practical, readers will find many usable insights to restore churches to health and vitality. In my opinion, it ranks in the top five books on the subject of church turnaround.

Gary L. McIntosh, PhD, professor, Talbot School of Theology,
Biola University, La Mirada, California

This book is the book you need. I make that statement without hesitation or reservation. With over 90 percent of American churches in need of revitalization, *Can These Bones Live?* is an incredible resource for leaders and church members to reverse the dire trends. The book is deeply biblical, immensely practical, and thoroughly encouraging. Thank you, Bill Henard. You have done a great service to churches around the world with this book.

Thom S. Rainer, president and CEO, LifeWay Christian Resources,
Nashville, Tennessee

Written by a veteran pastor who loves the local church, this book offers encouraging stories, practical steps, and useful resources for the church leader seeking to lead his church in revitalization. It is filled with Christian hope—a trusting assurance that God still brings new life to dying congregations. Read this work, and apply its insights in your church.

Chuck Lawless, PhD, VP of Graduate Studies and Ministry Centers,
Southeastern Seminary, Wake Forest, North Carolina,
and Global Theological Education Consultant,
International Mission Board

Yes, dry church bones can come alive, and Bill Henard tells us how. A straight-from-the-shoulder, down-to-earth call for revival I strongly recommend.

Robert E. Coleman, Distinguished Senior Professor of Evangelism and Discipleship, Gordon-Conwell Theological Seminary, Charlotte, North Carolina

Bill Henard is that rare combination of pastor, scholar, and leader who has been effectively used by God to revitalize several local churches over the course of his ministry. Now he has given to all of us who care about church vitality an indispensable guide on how struggling congregations can recapture their passion for God and His mission. As you read these pages you will find practical wisdom for pastors and churches written by one who affirms the full truthfulness of Scripture and the life-changing power of the Holy Spirit. I wish I could place this book in the hands of every seminary student preparing for the pastorate. I cannot recommend *Can These Bones Live?* highly enough.

Adam W. Greenway, PhD, Dean, Billy Graham School of Missions, Evangelism and Ministry, The Southern Baptist Theological Seminary

Some argue for prioritizing church planting by observing, "It is easier to give birth than to raise the dead." With perhaps eighty percent of our churches plateaued or declining, we not only must plant new churches but must seek to revitalize existing churches. Bill Henard's *Can These Bones Live?* is a superb resource on church revitalization. Filled with biblical and practical wisdom, this book will help guide a revitalization process in your local church. Read it. Digest it. Apply it.

Timothy K. Beougher, Associate Dean, Billy Graham School of Missions, Evangelism and Ministry, Billy Graham Professor of Evangelism and Church Growth, The Southern Baptist Theological Seminary

CAN
THESE
BONES
LIVE

BILL HENARD

CAN THESE BONES LIVE?

B&H
PUBLISHING GROUP

NASHVILLE, TENNESSEE

978-1-4336-8397-8

Published by B&H Publishing Group
Nashville, Tennessee

Dewey Decimal Classification: 269
Subject Heading: CHURCH RENEWAL \ EVANGELISTIC WORK \
CHURCH

2 3 4 5 6 7 8 • 22 21 20 19 18

To my grandchildren.
I cannot express the joy that God has brought
to my life through my children's children:

Ashlyn
Alex
Laurel
Ivy

Contents

Acknowledgments

I n any undertaking, it is important to acknowledge those who have made essential contributions. Without others, I could not have completed this project. I want to thank my church staff for their help in gathering some of the information I needed for this book. My ministry assistant, Melanie Booth, offered assistance and help whenever I asked. I am indebted to Dr. Jerry Sheveland, who gave permission to draw from some of his teaching material on plateaued churches. Finally, I am thankful for my editor, Devin Maddox, whose advice, critique, and encouragement proved invaluable to me.

I am grateful for each church that has permitted me to serve as their pastor. It is amazing what churches endure in allowing pastors to lead them. Porter Memorial Baptist Church has been especially patient and compassionate.

I love my family. I cannot imagine being in ministry without the love and support of my wife Judy, my children, Virginia, David, and Andy, and my grandchildren, Ashlyn, Alex, Laurel, and Ivy.

Ultimately, I am awed at the amazing grace of Christ. He never gives up on us. As we falter and fail, even in the church, Christ offers the forgiveness that can only be received through His sacrificial death.

Foreword

We face a triple crisis in the North American church today as we seek to influence a culture that is increasingly lost and indifferent to the things of God. First, our population continues to grow and become more diverse, yet we are not starting enough new churches to keep pace with that growth. Second, we are losing a shockingly high number of churches every year that simply close their doors and disappear. Third, even more of our existing churches have stopped being outwardly focused and are no longer lights for the gospel in their communities.

At the North American Mission Board where I serve, our mission is to help Southern Baptists push back lostness in North America. To do that, we need to close the gap between our number of churches and the growing population. That gap grew from one church for every thirty-eight hundred people in 1900 to one church for every sixty-two hundred today.

To close this gap, we want to help increase the church birth rate by helping Southern Baptists start fifteen thousand new churches over a ten-year period. But we also need to help decrease the church death rate.

If we simply start more churches but continue losing about a thousand a year—which is the current average among Southern Baptists—we will, at best, be treading water. At the same time, if increasing numbers of existing churches lose their effectiveness, you can see how our influence on the world will keep slipping.

Viewed through the lens of any research you look at, Southern Baptist churches are in the midst of a health crisis and have been for many years. We analyzed data from the Annual Church Profile (ACP) and found that between 2007 and 2012, only 27 percent of reporting SBC churches experienced growth. Forty-three percent were plateaued and 30 percent declined.

But our analysis looked at membership numbers. A study by the Leavell Center for Evangelism and Church Health at New Orleans Baptist Theological Seminary looked at worship attendance and found that in 2010 only 6.8 percent of SBC churches were healthy.

This is why we must make church revitalization a high priority. We can no longer settle for seeing so many of our churches slip away or lose their influence each year.

If you are pastoring a church in need of revitalization, I hope you will take encouragement from the powerful resource you hold in your hands. Bill Henard has compiled an exhaustive guide for helping you think through the personal and corporate journey you must embark on if your church is to return to healthier days.

As Bill points out, seeking God's presence must be the top priority, and that begins with a pastor's individual walk with the Lord. Put God first, follow His lead, and then let Him be responsible for the results. It's His church and, as much as you love it, He loves it even more.

—Kevin Ezell

Can These Bones Live?

The Old Testament is replete with stories of intrigue, with one of those narratives originating within the prophecies of Ezekiel. Depending on one's own eschatological leanings, Ezekiel's words offer a variety of interpretations. This fact is especially true in Ezekiel 37, the prophecy of the valley of dry bones.

Outside of his own personal biography, Ezekiel's life story is essentially unknown. He lived in the tumultuous times as Israel watched and experienced their destruction at the hands of the Babylonians. Ezekiel himself became a casualty of war, as he was taken captive most probably during the second of the three deportations. One immediately discovers the providence of God, as Ezekiel began his prophecies during his captivity. He offers the hope of the thirty-seventh chapter in response to the destruction of Jerusalem and the sacred temple. The die is now cast. (No pun is actually intended here in using this idiom, but one can imagine that if nothing changes, many churches are going to literally die.) Judgment has come, but God reveals Himself as the God of revitalization and resurrection.[1]

The question of the moment is the one asked by God of Ezekiel, "Can these bones live?" Ezekiel's answer resonates with most who love the church, "Lord GOD, only You know" (37:3). The prophecy specifically regards Israel's return from captivity. Many see this passage with a greater eschatological significance, relating it to Israel's gathering as converted believers in God's kingdom. Regardless of how one views the eschatological significance of this passage, two important ingredients are essential for Israel's return.

The first requirement necessitates the preaching of God's Word. God tells Ezekiel, "Prophesy concerning these bones" (37:4). As Ezekiel obeys, the Scripture unveils this magnificent vision of bones taking on tendons and flesh. Note carefully that the bones described are dry bones. These soldiers who died in battle were not afforded the privilege of a proper burial. They experienced the great disgrace of open decay. Yet God intervenes, and Ezekiel speaks to the bones.

The second standard for revitalization set by God involves the work of the Spirit. The word *breath* occurs in a variety of ways in this passage. That issue causes the reader to remain somewhat in the dark concerning its meaning as God says that He "will cause breath to enter you, and you will live" (37:5). The word for *breath* in the Hebrew (*ruah*) is actually translated as three different words in English, namely, *breath, wind,* and *spirit*. The writer resolves this question as God declares, "I will put My Spirit in you, and you will live" (37:14).[2]

In order for the church to be revived, it will demand a mighty work of God's Spirit. Following a particular methodology or program does not guarantee success. One might greatly desire for the church to revitalize and grow, but genuine church growth calls for more than personal passion. It requires the Spirit of God. Church revitalization begins with laying the foundation of God's Word as it is preached and followed through a movement of God's Spirit. The two are inseparably linked.

Can these bones live? Only God knows, yet He instills hope in those who desire to see the established church thrive and revive. Just as God miraculously returned Israel to her home, He can bring restoration to a declining, dying church.

1

Why Church Revitalization?

The first question that one must ask is, "Why is there such a great need for church revitalization?" The answer to that question is simple. At present, anywhere from thirty-five hundred to four thousand churches across denominational lines are closing their doors every year.[3] I have read that upwards of seven thousand churches shut down, but I have never seen any real research to justify these numbers. An article by Thom Rainer stated that as many as a hundred thousand American churches will close their doors over the next decade if nothing changes. In this blog post, Rainer listed eleven signs that a church was dying or already dead. These include:

1. The church refused to look like the community.
2. The church had no community-focused ministries.
3. Members became more focused on memorials.
4. The percentage of the budget for members' needs kept increasing.
5. There were no evangelistic emphases.
6. The members had more and more arguments about what *they* wanted.
7. With few exceptions, pastoral tenure grew shorter and shorter.
8. The church rarely prayed together.
9. The church had no clarity as to why it existed.

10. The members idolized another era.
11. The facilities continued to deteriorate.[4]

If Rainer's research is correct, he is predicting that ten thousand churches will close their doors annually over the next decade—a number that surpasses all present estimates. The fact that between 70 and 80 percent of churches are plateaued or are in decline also defends these calculations. Many of these churches will not be in existence in the next ten years.

Two positive issues thankfully surface in the midst of these discouraging numbers. First, a study published in the *Journal for the Scientific Study of Religion* concluded that only about 1 percent of American congregations are closing annually—a number, according to this report, that demonstrates one of the lowest mortality rates for any type of organization. The study was conducted by Duke University professor Mark Chaves, who began his study in 1998. His research revealed that only about ten out of a thousand religious congregations disband each year. The criteria for his research involved reexamining congregations he had originally studied through the *1998 National Congregations Study*. Chaves then reconnected with those congregations to determine how many of them were still active by holding regular services and maintaining other evidences of activity and ministry in 2005.

The one limiting issue within his research is the fact that he did not just evaluate evangelical or Christian churches. His investigation involved 1,230 churches, synagogues, and mosques, including those associated with the Jehovah's Witnesses, Lutheran, Protestant, Episcopal, and Roman Catholics, among others.[5] The fact that his research expanded beyond the Christian church might skew the numbers pertinent for this study somewhat. There were an estimated 314,000 Christian congregations in America as of 2010.[6] This particular research would imply a slightly lower number of congregations closing than what other research indicates. His findings, however, do give some encouragement at least for the present.

A second positive finding by Ed Stetzer reveals that around thirty-five hundred church plants launch every year. Stetzer also has reported that only about one-third of these church starts cease to exist by the fourth year of their launch. He writes,

Statistics randomly and regularly quoted have led many to believe that 80 percent of church plants fail in the first year. However, a recent study by the Center for Missional Research showed considerably more favorable results. Twelve denominations and networks participated in the study with over 1,000 church plants' status of existence determined. With more than 500 completed interviews, the study reveals that 99 percent of church plants survive the first year, 92 percent the second year, 81 percent the third year, and 68 percent the fourth year.[7]

While these statistics offer good news for the church world, the fact remains that, at best, the church is barely breaking even. We may have stemmed the tide regarding the total numbers in church closings, but if nothing changes, a tsunami of church deaths may overwhelm the Christian community. In fact, if Rainer's conclusions are accurate estimating that ten thousand churches will close each year over the next decade, we will once again be losing ground quickly.

These facts and many others explain clearly why church revitalization is so desperately needed. Some churches seemingly need to close and will, in spite of any attempts at saving them. Others certainly are salvageable. They may have lost their way and have lost their vision, but there is hope for the church.

Think of the words of Jesus for a moment. He is traveling through the region of Caesarea Philippi with His disciples. They are headed to the Mount of Transfiguration, a mountain I believe to be Mount Hermon in Syria, not too far away. It would be on Mount Hermon that Christ would be transfigured in front of Peter, James, and John. The word *transfigured* literally comes from the Greek word *metamorphoō*, suggesting a change in Christ's appearance. Craig Blomberg explains, "His skin and clothes shine with dazzling brilliance and whiteness, suggesting glory, sovereignty, and purity."[8] This inner circle received a glimpse into the deity of Christ. That coming fact plays an important role in the present situation with the disciples at Caesarea Philippi.

The region of Caesarea Philippi abounded with statues and idols to the various gods of Rome. More than 150 Roman gods existed, with twelve primary deities. Caesar Augustus had given the region to Herod the Great in 20 BC, who built a white marble temple in Paneas in honor of the emperor. Herod's son, Philip the tetrarch, inherited the land, greatly enlarged the city, and renamed it after Caesar in 2 BC. He added the name Philippi both to gain honor for himself and to distinguish this Caesarea from the one on the Mediterranean coast west of Jerusalem.

The background of Paneas originates in deep paganism. Pan was the Greek god, half man, half goat. He played the flute or the pipes, looking to see whom he might cause to be overcome with panic. Pan supposedly was born in a nearby cave that was also occupied by other deities during the winter months. The Temple of Augustus was actually built over the sight of this cave, with the grotto connecting to the back of the temple. A number of niches were carved into the rock next to the cave to hold the statues of various other gods. Next to the Temple of Augustus was the Temple to Zeus and Pan. To the left of these two temples was the Court of Pan and the Nymphs. In years prior to the building of the temple, the townspeople offered blood sacrifices, with the hope that Pan and the gods would accept these offerings. If received, the springs that ran through the back of the cave and into the Springs of Hermon would remain clear. If unaccepted, the springs would turn red with blood.

Now Jesus and His disciples are walking through this region. One can imagine that, in encountering the various idols and statues and with the known history of the region, questions and discussions arose regarding these icons. This assumed dialogue perhaps led to the questions asked by Jesus, "Who do people say that the Son of Man is?" (Matt. 16:13) and "Who do you say that I am?" (Matt. 16:15). *Here are all of these statues to these gods, who do you think that I am?* Through that question, Simon Peter reacts with, conceivably, the most important, single statement made in Scripture. Peter responds, "You are the Messiah, the Son of the living God!" (Matt. 16:16). Jesus then replies with this explication, "Simon son of Jonah, you are blessed because flesh and blood did not reveal this to you, but My Father in heaven. And I also say to you that you are Peter, and on this rock I will build My church, and the forces of Hades will not overpower it" (Matt. 16:17–18).

The disciples had been looking at all of these idols and statues and temples, all dedicated to dead gods of human imagination. Yet the citizens of Rome immersed themselves into the worship of these false gods, leaving them with a lostness enshrouded by canards. Could it be that

Jesus offered this declaration at some point after they had passed by the Temple of Augustus? Many scholars, including myself, wonder if Jesus was not directly referring to the cave of Pan as symbolic of the forces of Hades or the gates of hell. The cave would certainly have made an incredible object lesson. Here, according to pagan legend, sits the entrance to the abyss, the very gates of hell. Yet Christ declares that even death itself (the Greek word He uses is *Hades* not *Gehenna*) will not overpower the church. The church belongs to Jesus; she is His church. She exists as His bride, and Christ clarifies that the church will survive. Whatever Satan throws at her, she will survive.

The church has a future and a hope. Before any one of us can go forward with the idea of church revitalization, we must arrive at that conclusion. It is more than research, location, statistics, negatives, the past, the present, the people, or the naysayers. In order for anyone to initiate revitalization effectively into the local church, that person must believe Christ's promises about His church. I love the church because she is a survivor!

Beginning Steps: Assumptions and Presumptions

While affirming that Christ will build His church, the church revitalizer must begin with some particular assumptions about church growth and health. I call them assumptions and presumptions because we must begin with some particulars that lead us to believe that the church can survive and then lay claim to those presumptions and make them our own. Again, we may be like Ezekiel and wonder if these bones can live. Yet, at the same time, we must approach church revitalization with the presumption that God has a plan for the church, and then we make those presuppositions our own. If we really do not believe that a church can survive, it probably will not even if it could. We will not put in the effort and energy. So start with these presumptions and make them your own.

God Wants the Church to Revitalize

That statement may seem a little redundant, but I have heard both pastors and laypeople over the years make statements that they believed it might be better for a church to die than to change. Many times these statements occurred in the context of a discussion regarding relocation or a major strategy change, but I find it disturbing that any of us would believe that a church should die. Do churches die? Of course they do. That issue offers the primary motivation for this book. Should churches die? If we believe that the church belongs to Jesus, then to offer an answer in the affirmative becomes a much more difficult conclusion. Therefore, I start with this presumption: God wants the church to grow. It is His will and plan. It is a presumption that does not mean that the church is without challenges. The church has always had challenges.

Look at the early church in Jerusalem, from its very beginnings in the book of Acts. The church began with at least three thousand members. It grew in numbers, first as individuals were being added to the church (Acts 2:47), and eventually to the point that Luke just said, "the number of the disciples was multiplying" (Acts 6:1). Those of us who love to see the church grow enjoy reading those words and long to see that growth happen again. It can, but we must believe that it can. Even a church that has been in decline for a decade or more can grow and become a Great Commission church again because God wants the church collective and the local church to grow. Fulfilling the Great Commission is God's will.

Church Health Results in Church Revitalization

In church circles today, many writers and bloggers on the church have moved away from the church growth terminology in favor of church health. I am drawn back to classic books on church growth by Donald McGavran, *Understanding Church Growth*, Thom Rainer, *The Book of Church Growth*, Gene Mims, *Kingdom Principles for Church Growth*, and even C. B. Hogue's, *I Want My Church to Grow*. Now books that deal with growth address these issues through more contemporary models, recognizing that church growth must be healthy. Mark Dever's *Nine Marks of a Healthy Church*, Stephen Macchia's *Becoming a Healthy Church*, and even to some degree Colin Marshall and Tony Payne's *The Trellis and the Vine*, all demonstrate this paradigm shift from church growth to church health.

An honest appraisal of modern church growth methods affirms the need for this perspective. In our world today, we have learned how to grow churches through a variety of means. We have become so concise and advanced in our methodology, technology, and programming that a church leader can grow a church and quite possibly never have to mention the name of Jesus. Through research, we have learned what the unchurched world wants, and we have built churches that have gotten out of balance in their approach in catering to what people do not like about church. As a result, many pastors are fearful of church revitalization because of the onslaught of blogs, ads, and publications that promote "a new church for people who do not like church" as though there is something anathema about the established church.

Please do not misunderstand this point. The established church needs to embrace change, but we should not be fearful of the so-called traditional church. In my conversations with church planters over the years, I have asked them about tradition. Without exception, these individuals have all affirmed that, within seven years of founding their churches, deep-seeded traditions became the norm and had to be addressed. Therefore, if we are drawn to church planting rather than church revitalization because we reject tradition, we will be leaving our churches about every four to seven years. Better reasons must exist for why we plant churches and why we revitalize churches.

Look at the Scriptures for a moment. In Paul's second letter to Timothy, he addresses a variety of issues this young pastor faces and will face. Nero's persecution was moving to a fevered pitch, resulting in Paul's arrest and his second imprisonment. As he writes this letter from his dungeon cell, waiting for his martyrdom, he admonishes Timothy to be faithful to "preach the word" (2 Tim. 4:2 ESV). One of the reasons that a faithfulness to God's Word was so essential was because "the time will come when they will not tolerate sound doctrine, but according to their own desires, will multiply teachers for themselves because they have an itch to hear something new" (2 Tim. 4:3). I often wonder if we are not living in those times. The fact remains, not all church growth is healthy church growth. Not all churches that are growing experience biblical church growth. Drawing a crowd is not the same as growing a church.

Other criteria must be present to evaluate the church besides just numbers. Numbers continue to be extremely important. For the same reasons that we stepped away from the church growth nomenclature because it appeared that all it emphasized was numbers, we must be faithful to apply that same standard to contemporary church methods. Thus, church revitalization becomes a viable means of church growth because it necessitates church health. Many churches fall into decline because they have become unhealthy, so a prospective pastor will never accomplish church turnaround if church health is not achieved. The two go inseparably together.

I googled "Characteristics of a Healthy Church" and got over one million hits. Time would not permit me to read all one million results, but the lists varied from three to twelve distinctives. Dever obviously addresses nine marks. Macchia identifies ten characteristics for a healthy church. I believe that most, if not all, of these traits are discovered in Luke's account of the early church. Look at Acts 2:41–47 and an immediate recognition of healthy church practices emerges. Take note of these identifying characteristics of church health:

An Authoritative View of Scripture. Simon Peter's sermon was filled with Old Testament quotes. Once the church was established, the Scripture declares, "So those who accepted his message were baptized . . . and they devoted themselves to the apostles' teaching" (Acts 2:41–42). The New Testament obviously had not been written yet, but soon copies would be circulated, beginning with the Gospels, Paul's letters to the churches of Galatia and Thessalonica, and James's epistle. The apostles' words were ones of authority. In order for a church to develop and maintain good health, it must be committed to God's Word as its authority for both what the church believes and how it practices its polity and faith. Every method, program, and change must be evaluated on its biblical content, not just on its effectiveness.

A Focus on Discipleship and Small Groups. While they "devoted themselves to the apostles' teaching," they also "broke bread from house to house" (Acts 2:42, 46), indicating a commitment to discipleship but also to small groups. The evidence of a belief in God's Word is that it affects our lives, our daily decisions, and our entire beings.

A Strong Emphasis on Biblical Preaching. Simon Peter's first act once the Holy Spirit had moved was to preach. As they "devoted themselves to the apostles' teaching" and "to meeting together in the temple complex" (Acts 2:42, 46), these activities certainly involved preaching and evangelism. One of the problems that the church is facing today is a loss of the prophetic voice. Preaching has become secondary, even nonessential, in some church circles and methods. Yet the public proclamation of God's Word remains a sign of church health. Healthy believers love biblical preaching. They always have and always will.

A Connection to the Community. We might use the term *relevant* at this point. I am not sure that the early church tried to be relevant, but a look at the text shows that their message spoke to the hearts of the people. Luke says that they had "favor with all the people" (Acts 2:47). While this almost universal favor would be short-lived (read Acts 4 for an explanation), the fact persists that the message of the gospel continued to meet people's needs. We must not forget that important detail. Being relevant is far more than being cool. Biblical relevance demands a gospel connection.

A Vigorous Commitment to Prayer. Acts 2:42 tells us that the early church was devoted to, among other things, prayer. In our churches today, if there is a ministry that is so greatly neglected and taken for granted, it has to be prayer. We call Wednesday nights "Prayer meeting," yet we rarely pray. It has been my sad discovery that Christians find it uncomfortable to pray with one another. I conclude that the reason probably stems from the fact that we have not accomplished the other characteristics of church health. Therefore, we do not pray. If a pastor asked me advice on what to do first in accepting a very unhealthy church in need of revitalization but not ready for change, my response would be, "Preach the Word, Pastor the People, Practice Personal Evangelism, and Prioritize Congregational Prayer" (see chapter 4 for more detail).

A Dedication to Genuine Ministry. Acts 2:43–44 explains this process. Historians record how following Christ became a costly decision for the first Christians. Paul would later ask for an offering to be taken for the church in Jerusalem by the other churches under his care (1 Cor. 16:1–4; 2 Cor. 8:1–9:15; Rom. 15:14–32) because of the loss these believers suffered. Early on, the church was committed to meeting the needs of its members. I emphasize the words *genuine ministry* because this practice is not about "taking care of us." The dying church oftentimes becomes incredibly introverted and protected so that all of its money and time is spent on itself. Genuine ministry does not intend to isolate; it means to provide.

A Submission to the Work of the Holy Spirit. The question that every church must ask is, "Are we growing because God is moving or because our methods are working?" God very well may be using the methods that a church employs, but we have learned how to draw crowds through our music, methods, and marketing. We must be honest at this point. We will be careful to baptize our work with the words, "God gets all the credit," when in fact He may not have been involved in the work at all. Healthy churches are ones that experience growth through the power of the Holy Spirit. The Spirit's presence and movement are evident, not only in the preaching, but in the lives of the people.

A Practice of Personal Evangelism. Evangelism seems to be a natural response to all the other things they were doing in the church. Obviously, they were brand-new Christians and were excited about their newfound faith. Churches and Christians that have been around awhile often lose or forget about that excitement. It is interesting that the exact methods of evangelism are not promoted as much as the result, as Luke says, "And every day the Lord added to them those who were being saved" (Acts 2:47). Luke emphasizes the work of God far more than the work of humans. Genuine salvation always reflects that fact. What I have discovered in all the years that I have been teaching evangelism and practicing evangelism is that methods change but the results do not. God is still in the business of saving sinners. A healthy church is not defined by how it does evangelism. It is marked by the fact that it does evangelism and sees the results of that work.

Principles of Revitalization and Growth Can Be Applied to Any Church, in Any Situation

The emphasis here is not on methodology. Methods change and methods may be applicable only to a particular locale or demographic. The basic biblical principles of church health already mentioned can be implemented in any church, at any time, and in any place. Pastors make the fatal mistake of believing that, because a method works in California or Chicago, it will work in Oswego or Bunion. Most of us have probably made this mistake. What matters is finding what works, not using the latest and greatest method. Be careful to know the demographic of your people. What you particularly like may not be what meets their needs or reaches people.

Church Revitalization Must Be a Work of God's Spirit

If God desires for the church to be revitalized, He certainly can provide the power for that result to materialize. Thus, if we desire for that work to remain, it must be a movement of God. God uses people and structures. He affirms programs and mission statements. I do not believe that God is anti-methodology, yet all of those things are irrelevant if God's Spirit does not move. In fact, many of the obstacles that a pastor faces in revitalization are overcome simply through the power of the Holy Spirit. It is amazing what happens when people, including pastors, get right with God.

Church Revitalization Occurs Because of Good Planning

A pastor needs to have a plan in hand in order to see church revitalization occur. It must be a work of God, but God oftentimes uses human means to bring about His purposes. He uses the art of preaching to communicate His Word. He uses methods of evangelism to bring people to faith in Christ, and He uses plans and processes to position a church to experience revitalization.

Church Revitalization Succeeds Because of Servant Leadership

One can find a great deal of material written on the issue of leadership. I am reluctant to accept any statement that says that everything rises and falls on leadership. That fact may be true in some venues, but the church is not a secular institution or business. What I would encourage pastors to pursue is not leadership in itself but servant leadership.

In reading the Gospels, and even the entire New Testament, the issue of leadership is not addressed as much as, not just the quality of service, but of being a slave of Christ. John MacArthur wrote a book back in 2010 entitled *Slave: The Hidden Truth about Your Identity in Christ.* In the book, he offers this perspective:

> Though the word *slave* (*doulos* in Greek) appears 124 times in the original text, it is correctly translated only once in the King James. Most of our modern translations do only slightly

better. . . . True Christianity is not about adding Jesus to *my* life. Instead, it is about devoting myself completely to *Him*—submitting wholly to His will and seeking to please Him above all else. It demands dying to self and following the Master, no matter the cost. In other words, to be a Christian is to be Christ's *slave*.[9]

The perspective of Jesus best fits at this point. In Philippians 2:5–8, Paul reminds us of the deity of Jesus in a way that might seem unfamiliar to some and, perhaps, even unconventional. Paul writes,

> Make your own attitude that of Christ Jesus, who, existing in the form of God, did not consider equality with God as something to be used for His own advantage. Instead He emptied Himself by assuming the form of a slave, taking on the likeness of men. And when He had come as a man in His external form, He humbled Himself by becoming obedient to the point of death—even to death on a cross.

Of the multitude of thought presented in this passage, I want to focus on two. First, Jesus existed *in the form of God*. The word *form* is the Greek word *morphē*, a word that "describes not simply external appearance or behaviour but also that which inwardly corresponds (or is expected to correspond) to the outward."[10] Most scholars look to this word to mean that Christ was not just like God, He was fully and completely God. As much and as full as God the Father is God, Jesus the Son is God. Taking that fact into consideration, the text then tells us that Christ also "emptied Himself by assuming the form of a slave" (2:7). I am not going to get into the debate here about the theory of *kenosis* versus the *hypostatic union* of Christ (I personally choose the latter over the former), but what we understand about this particular passage is that Jesus literally became a man and literally took on the *morphē* of a servant. He did not just appear to be a slave. He in all ways and forms became a slave (*doulos*), from the inside of His character to His behavior in the world.

A primary issue facing the ministry and the church is the need for genuine humility. Sometimes churches fall into decline because they hold to an arrogance that developed out of prestige and position. Most of the time, these perspectives have arisen from years gone by, but they are prevalent nonetheless. As a church lives in the past and upon its past successes and prominence, it may reject any idea of revitalization as something unneeded. The church seems to be repeating the mistakes of the past. Look at Israel. She had been told by the prophets that judgment was coming, yet she believed that judgment would not come because she was Israel, the people of God. Yet, judgment came to the Northern Kingdom. Amos declared, "Listen and testify against the house of Jacob—this is the declaration of the Lord GOD, the God of Hosts. I will punish the altars of Bethel on the day I punish Israel for its crimes; the horns of the altar will be cut off and fall to the ground" (Amos 3:13–14).

Just over one hundred years later, judgment would also come to the Southern Kingdom. Jeremiah would literally be standing in the temple, pleading with Zedekiah to repent and trust God (see Jer. 38:14ff). Because of fear and pride, however, Zedekiah refused. Nebuchadnezzar was at that very moment heading toward Jerusalem, but the king would not relent. Pride overcame him, as it had the kingdom of Judah, and Jerusalem fell. The last thing that Zedekiah saw was the death of his sons. His eyes were gouged out, and he was carried off to Babylon (Jer. 39:6–7).

Pastors face that same temptation of arrogance and pride. From the young seminarian who either rejects the established church because he has grown beyond the traditions held by congregations to the matured pastor who has reached the pinnacle of his profession, arrogance permeates the ministry (myself included). I cannot tell you the number of times that I have been in denominational meetings, both local and national, and the air is thick with personality. I have watched as leaders ignore one person because that individual "can't get me where I want to be" to where they fall all over themselves to ensure that someone else knows of their presence. Sadly, many of them do not even recognize what they are doing or why. If someone confronted them about arrogance, they would be amazed at that accusation. I believe that typical response is an example of how strong pride is in our lives and most of us find ourselves at that juncture. We struggle with our egos.

Therefore, talking about leadership appeals to us. We want to be leaders, admired and respected by all. We want to influence and direct. We desire recognition and responsibility. To be honest, it has to take some amount of self-confidence to make it in the ministry. A pastor has to believe in what God has called him to do. He has to be able to wake up on Monday morning after a terrible Sunday and continue on because he believes in what he is doing. A lack of conviction at this point becomes a deadly proposition, especially in dealing with revitalization.

I want to propose, though, a different paradigm. Instead of needing leaders, the church needs servant-leaders, ones who model the mind-set of Christ. We have to believe in what God has called us to do. We need confidence in God and in our own abilities. That confidence, however, needs to be balanced with us seeing ourselves as Christ's slaves. We are called to serve the church, not for the church to serve us. We are chosen to lead the church as servants who invest in the welfare and the future of the church, not the padding of our résumés. I have often wondered if one of the reasons that we are not seeing God move as we wish He would is because of the undeniable presence of pride in the life of Christians.

Basic Qualifications

If you are going to take the challenge to tackle church revitalization, how should you prepare yourself? What would be some necessary personal and biblical prerequisites that would be essential for you as the servant-leader of the church?

An Absolute Dependence upon the Holy Spirit

In spite of any revitalization project or method that you might follow, without the Holy Spirit our efforts are frustrating and will be fruitless. It is extremely important to understand how God uses *means* to bring about His program. We recognize the absolute sovereignty of our Savior Jesus (Phil. 2:5–11). Skeptics may try to cast doubt, but, in my opinion, no question exists as to His rule and reign. In His sovereignty, though, God has chosen to use people, programs, and methods to carry out His work. Our conclusion must be out of those facts that Jesus is not bound to produce results just because we implement the right method or follow the right program. Remember this truth: church revitalization occurs because of the empowerment of the Holy Spirit, not just because of our efforts.

A Consistent Spiritual Revitalization in Your Own Life

In understanding how God uses people to accomplish His tasks and the connection with the Holy Spirit's power, we must pursue diligently a consistent, personal spiritual growth formation in our own lives. One of the things that I have learned in ministry is that a pastor can become accomplished enough in methodology that he forgets his own spiritual growth. He can preach well-crafted sermons and do needs-based ministry and not be walking with Christ himself. One might not draw that conclusion or believe that it is possible, but considering the power of God's Word and His promises, some pastors can see some results in spite of their own shortsightedness. In all honesty, sometimes pastors are successful because of their personalities and abilities. They would succeed whether they are selling Jesus or selling soap.

Eventually the lack of spiritual growth will catch up to all of us. This fact is especially true in church revitalization. A church located in a prime area with little or no competition would probably have to have people stationed at the front door with shotguns to keep it from growing (although in today's culture, we might begin seeing even these churches struggle). Church revitalization originates from a different breed. No church revitalization project will be easy. Therefore, the pastor must be involved in a daily, personal study and application of Scripture.

One of the mistakes that many pastors make is to assume that sermon preparation equals personal Bible study. While it is true that a pastor gains greatly from a systematic and expositional study of Scripture in the preparation of sermons, a great deal of difference exists between personal Bible study and sermon preparation.

- **Sermon Prep is a required task; Personal Study is a volunteer action**
- **Sermon Prep applies to the masses; Personal Study applies to the student**
- **Sermon Prep results from the overflow; Personal Study creates the overflow**
- **Sermon Prep originates primarily out of what others have said about Scripture; Personal Study begins from a personal encounter with Scripture**

- **Sermon Prep results in the applause of people; Personal Study results in the affirmation of God**

The list could go on. I am not saying that some crossover does not exist between the two disciplines. Nor am I saying that sermon preparation serves as an unimportant or a menial duty, but what I know is that personal Bible study becomes essential both to the task of sermon preparation and to the success of church revitalization. On the seminary level, I have taught preaching, evangelism, and church revitalization among other subjects. In all of my classes, I highly encourage students to be involved in a daily quiet time with Scripture that is not connected to any other responsibility, whether related to school or church. A Christian will never learn to be dependent upon the Holy Spirit if a personal quiet time is not a priority.

Personal, spiritual revitalization means exactly that idea—personal revitalization. Pastoral ministry at every level fosters incredibly draining experiences and encounters. If the pastor neglects personal growth, this oversight probably will result in discouragement, depression, and an eventual dropout. Here are some depressing statistics:

- 1,400 pastors in America leave the ministry monthly
- Less than 20% of churches recognized or appreciated their pastor in some way annually
- Only 15% of churches in the United States are growing and just 2.2% of those are growing by conversion growth
- 10,000 churches in America disappeared in a five-year period
- The number of people in America that do not attend church has doubled in the past 15 years
- The vast majority of churches have an attendance of less than 75
- In 70% of the churches in America, the pastor is the only full-time staff person
- 23% of church attendees say they attend a small group for growth or accountability
- Only 65% of Americans donate to a place of worship
- Only 60% of Christians say they are deeply committed to their faith
- Only one-third of church attendees believe that they have a responsibility to share their faith

- 26% of Evangelicals believe that salvation can be earned
- In his book, *Who Shall Lead Them?* Larry Witham said, "20% of US churches have no future."[11]

All the statistics are discouraging until we realize that the hope for the church comes from the empowerment of the Holy Spirit and the willingness of the pastor to be used as a means of revitalization. To be this utilized pastor demands personal, daily revitalization. Before a pastor initializes a program for revitalization, some simple steps need to be followed. I recognize that these steps may seem to be rather unsophisticated and even condescending. One would think that every Christian knows how to do a quiet time, but the fact is many of us do not. This detail happens to be especially true in ministry, so allow me the privilege to suggest these ideas:

1. Set aside a specific, uninterrupted time for Bible study.
2. Use a Bible and notebook that will be used only for this study. Acquire a Bible where notes can easily be written in the margins, on the pages, and in the back.
3. Utilize a devotional guide that will help you in a systematic or topical study of Scripture. Suggestions are *Daily Walk* published by Walk Through the Bible Ministries or *LifeWalk* published by LifeWay Press.
4. Put together a spiral-bound prayer notebook in which daily and weekly prayers can be recorded and tabbed when answered. Pray daily for your ministry and immediate family members. On each day of the week, have other specific requests that relate to your church, church members, missions and specific missionaries, other family members, nonbelievers, other believers, and a day just for thanksgiving. Put these ideas into categories that you follow Monday through Sunday. By following a plan like this one, a daily prayer routine will not become rote or repetitive.
5. Include a specific time that relates to your own confession of sin, need for personal revival and revitalization, and the need for your church and ministry. Keep an ongoing list of church needs that relate to revitalization.
6. Do not let anything get in the way of your time for revitalization.

I am convinced that, with all of the discouragements and disappointments that pastors face, the one resolve that creates a steady sense of expectation comes from personal revitalization. One cannot revitalize the church if personal pessimism becomes the norm.

A God-Sized Vision

Take time to study the Scripture concerning the makeup of the church. Many excellent books have been written that develop a clear ecclesiology and practice for the church. Look beyond these books and ask, "What would God want for my church?" What do you believe God wants to see happen and what do you want to see happen in your church? Out of these questions, formulate a vision. If no obstacles existed, what characteristics would define the church? Even if obstacles occur (which they will), what basic, foundational, and biblical values are essential and nonnegotiable? It is very important that these values and this vision be written down so that they can be articulated at the proper time. Know where you want to go before you begin the journey and make sure that it is something that demands the attention of God.

A Compassion for God's People

Never forget that the people you are serving are God's people. An easy temptation is to see people as objects or projects rather than as the redeemed of God. Remember that the pastor will answer for how he leads God's people (Heb. 13:17). Therefore, make the commitment early to be patient, understanding, and sensitive to the church. Most of them will never be where you are in developing vision and foresight for the church. That reason alone is why you are the leader. As the leader, though, do not run so far ahead of the church that you are no longer leading. Love people and determine ahead of time to give them time to follow.

A Commitment to Integrity

The ends do not always justify the means, even when the process results in something biblical. Unfortunately, pastors allow the desire to grow the church to open the way for all types of compromises. No one can really say what the results will be from a church that has refused to be salt and light and a people who have bought into the idea that being like the world means reaching the world. We have seen the result of fallen pastors and failed churches. We know that the church will survive and prevail, but what will be lost in the meantime if integrity does not guide the pastor? Therefore, without regret, be a person of integrity.

Conclusion

One of the opening screens on the NCAA Football video game has the voice of Brad Nessler telling players to "buckle up your chinstraps." His point is well taken. Church revitalization is not a task to be undertaken lightly. Some pastors need to be out planting churches. Others have skill sets that more easily match healthy, growing churches. Nevertheless, there are those individuals who recognize the need, possess the passion, and have the courage to see the established church survive and thrive. Truth is, regardless of the present state of any church, revitalization in some form will be necessary at some point. Therefore, it is essential that every church leader learn the expertise of revitalizing the church. So buckle up. Church revitalization offers an exciting ride.

CHAPTER

2

Assessment

Essentially there are two common scenarios in church revitalization. The first involves a pastor who interviews with and accepts the call to shepherd a local church in need of revitalization. The second is an individual who is already serving a church in need of revitalization. Both possess similarities and differences, yet the possibilities abound for a successful project in bringing renewal to the church. It requires asking good questions and making good preparations.

The first step is assessment. While no pastor should ever decide on accepting a position based solely on a church's potential, he needs to know "what he is getting into" before accepting a church or seeking to initiate changes within the congregation. As a pastor, you need to be open to the leadership of the Holy Spirit. If God says "Go," you go regardless. Being aware of the particulars of the situation, however, never hurts.

A great little book to read about assessment is John Kotter's *Our Iceberg Is Melting*. Kotter serves at the Harvard Business School. A very simple read, the book tells a make-believe story of a colony of penguins living on an iceberg in the Antarctic. While everything looks good on top of the iceberg, below the surface, evidence mounts that a catastrophe is about to occur. The story unfolds with how the colony leaders resist change and ignore the signs, even to the point to declare in absolute denial that the iceberg is not melting.[12] One thought gleaned from this book is the importance of assessment. Everything can look good throughout the initial meetings with committees and even during the "honeymoon" season. Yet the iceberg is melting, and if no one takes the time to assess the underlying problems, a great disaster is about to take place and the church dies.

The Interview Process

I am very much aware of the fact that some who read this book may be in a system whereby a board or a bishop makes pastoral appointments. Knowing these kinds of situations, the prospective pastor can still ask good questions that can be helpful both for him and for his congregation. In this section, though, I want to deal primarily with pastors who are called by church search committees rather than through an appointment process. The entire book can actually serve as an assessment tool, as the prospective pastor can evaluate the church's past and statistics in light of the eleven reasons why churches fall into decline.

The Big Lie

Not wishing to burst anyone's bubble, but the fact is in most cases, the pastoral search process is a big lie. It is much like dating. Two people, in some form or fashion, find themselves attracted to each other, and one contacts the other for an official date. The guy wants desperately to impress the girl, so he actually takes a shower and uses soap. He combs his hair and puts on deodorant. While on the date, he watches his manners and does not reveal the real self who sits around the house in sweatpants, rarely even brushing his teeth (not to mention other things for which guys are known).

The girl's makeup is perfect, her outfit matches without a single conflict, and she barely eats because that is what girls do. Politeness permeates the evening, but upon arriving at home, she goes back to being whatever she was before the date commenced. This practice continues on both parts for quite a while, perhaps even until the wedding day. Then the morning after the honeymoon arrives. Bad breath, bad hair, and bad habits are observed. Now the real relationship begins.

During the pastor search process, both parties present themselves at their best. The church search team does not particularly want the prospective pastor to see the church's "dirty laundry." They speak of the best of the best. I do not believe that committees intentionally lie about their particular situation. Sometimes they do not understand the dire need of their church, or they have reached a point of desperation whereby they have concluded that, if the pastor knows about the church's problems, he will not accept their invitation to serve at their church. Therefore, they avoid discussions regarding finances, staff, buildings, and neighborhoods. They divert questions away from the negative and move the conversation to the positive.

Questions to Ask

Understanding how these things occur, as a prospective pastor, one must be extremely careful in the interview process. Do not completely determine the acceptance or rejection of the call based solely on problems or challenges, but be aware of them. It is wise, however, to *know your challenges before you step into the pastorate.*

Here is a list of questions that should be asked in the interview process:

1. "If I come to be your pastor, what is your personal expectation of me? What do you want to see me do?"

   As a prospective pastor, you need to understand the investment that the search committee has in you. As a result, many of them will have personal expectations of the pastor beyond the expectations of the church. Facts show that oftentimes members of the search committee will end up leaving the church because their personal expectations were not met.

2. "To whom does the congregation look for leadership or approval? Who leads the church?"

   The pastor wants to be the leader, but oftentimes the congregation looks to someone else for leadership. The pastor needs to know who this person/these people are. Read John Maxwell's book *The 21 Irrefutable Laws of*

Leadership, particularly his story about Claude in Law 5, for an understanding of this principle.[13] The goal of this information is not for you to find out who leads so that you might manipulate a relationship with that person, but so that you will be aware of your challenges. Remember that leadership is earned, not demanded, in the church.

3. "Is there any one thing that you would not be willing to do even if it would mean that your church would grow (obviously as long as it is biblical, ethical, and moral)?"

Churches have sacred cows, and the prospective pastor needs to be aware of these. This particular question will probably need to be pressed and restated. The members of the committee will probably state that they are willing to make any change if it will help them to grow. The problem comes when they might not realize that a change needs to happen in a particular area of which they are fond or involved. Change is extremely difficult. No one likes change, not even pastors!

4. "What did you like and dislike about your previous pastors? What were some of their biggest mistakes? What were some of their greatest successes?"

Obviously, a pastor does not want to repeat mistakes, but it is also true that what the congregation might perceive as a mistake was more of personal dislike. You want to know the successes because a wise pastor will learn to build upon the successes of the past.

5. "Is there a particular topic that could be addressed in a sermon that would be totally unacceptable by the congregation?"

This question will assist in discovering some of the hidden moral or political issues with which the congregation deals at present or in the past. Most churches want to see themselves as conservative, but their personal views on certain moral or biblical issues will be enlightening.

6. "What was the subject of your most contentious business meeting? How do you normally conduct your business meetings?"

Depending on the polity of the church, most churches make at least some decisions through a business setting. One can discover the atmosphere of the church by understanding how members conduct themselves while discussing the needs of the church. A greater understanding into the congregation's perspective of pastoral leadership is also gained depending upon how involved the congregation wants the pastor to be during its business sessions.

7. "What is your perspective on how the church spends money?"

Money offers one of the most volatile insights into the church's future and past problems.

8. "How have the church finances fluctuated over the past five years?"

A prospective pastor will want to examine the church budget, expenses, and debt at least over the last five years, if possible. One can gain a glimpse into what the church has considered to be important, and what they have neglected.

9. "What are some of the times that you consider that you have grown spiritually, and what are you doing now to grow in your walk with Christ?"

Be careful in asking these questions, making sure that you have shared the answers for your own personal walk first. One suggestion would be to have them write out these answers if they would prefer. Normally, the search committee is a cross-section of people from the congregation, who represent those who are the most spiritual. That fact, however, is not always true. At a later time, I will be discussing the stakeholders and powerbrokers in the church. Sometimes these leaders do not want to make these decisions because of the fallout if things do not go well. Therefore they will lead through others. It is important that you know where your leadership is spiritually. Being a leader does not necessarily equate with being deeply spiritual.

10. "What is your personal vision or dream for the church? What would you desire to see happen in terms of worship, discipleship, and evangelism/missions?"

> The question serves the purpose of aiding the pastor in discerning the current direction of the church. If the church needs revitalization, that fact should be noticeable in the dreams of the committee. If an absence exists in recognizing the need for revitalization, this response will give the prospective pastor insight into the general perspective of the church. They may need revitalization but they do not know that they need revitalization, a reality that presents its own set of challenges.

Included with these particular questions should be discussions relating to the history of the church, the specific theological leanings of the committee and the congregation, the church staff and relationship expectations and supervision, compensation, and questions regarding church governance. All of these factors play a part in assisting a prospective pastor to understand the challenges before him and to be able to plot out a course for church revitalization.

The Established Pastor

Another recognized scenario stems from the individual who has served a particular church for some years but now recognizes that the obstacles he faces originate more out of a need for revitalization than just the ordinary struggles that every church faces. While he has obviously moved beyond the interview process, this particular situation can be very advantageous. First, the established pastor has developed rapport with his congregation. Trust has occurred, especially if he has walked through any particular crisis with the church and has stayed rather than bailing out to another church. He knows the community and the particulars of additional obstacles facing the church and its growth and health.[14]

Having these advantages, a suggested process for the established pastor would be to put together a revitalization team or committee that can help in evaluating the church's need for revitalization. Some churches already have a strategic planning, long-range planning, or leadership team, any of which would serve this process well. It would be advisable for the pastor to handpick this team, if possible, putting together people from a cross-section of ages, economics, experiences, and lengths of membership. In my opinion, this process would be the most desirable, yet I recognize that some churches may not allow the pastor this particular privilege. Nevertheless, a team of people would be greatly advantageous in evaluating the church's current situation and in leading the church through change. The same questions need to be asked as with a prospective pastor. Advantageously, the established pastor and the leadership team will be better equipped to find the answers.

Throughout this book, most of the suggestions or evaluations will be directed at the new pastor who is interviewing with or who arrives on a fresh church field. Nevertheless, the established pastor can apply all of those principles to the church. In fact, the established pastor most probably will have already recognized some of the problems and obstacles and will be a few steps ahead of the new pastor. The recommendations made in this book should aid him in formulating a vision and strategic plan for bringing about revitalization.

Stakeholder Symmetry

Tom Cheney, Carl George, Robert Logan, and Gary McIntosh, among others, have all taught or written on the idea of stakeholders in the church. The concept is that a number of people, both inside and outside of the church, have an investment in what the church does and accomplishes. *Effectively navigating the stormy waters of revitalization demands that the pastor understand these investors.* They come in three primary categories.

Investors Inside of the Church

Throughout the makeup of the church organization, one finds individuals and groups who have something invested and at stake in the church. Tom Cheney says that "these could be as low on an organizational chart as ushers and as high as full-time professional staff."[15] When a church has plateaued or is in decline, people point fingers of accusation. These indictments become a major obstacle for the established pastor, as someone has to be blamed for the decline. The new pastor will find that the investors inside the church may be suspicious of any ideas he might suggest. Therefore, if the pastor does not understand these investors, he may be in deep trouble, because one of the most difficult parts of church revitalization occurs when trying to initiate change in a church that struggles with issues of trust, suspicion, and blame. No one likes change. We are all creatures of habit in one form or another.

Keep that idea in mind when initiating church revitalization. People resist change simply because it is much easier to stay the same, fearing a loss of their present way of life, a state that they enjoy. They are oblivious to the true condition of the church and do not see a need for the church to revitalize or grow.

Carl George, in the book he coauthored with Robert Logan entitled *Leading and Managing Your Church,* presented the idea of a berry-bucket theory, drawing from a practice used by his grandfather in distributing his buckets of berries for consumption. George utilized this idea to categorize those investors in the church who hold claim to the power and future of the church. In this analogy, George identifies two primary groups, with two subgroups under each major grouping. The theory says that the makeup of the church's membership includes people both older and younger than the pastor who were members before the pastor began his service. With these former members, or formerberries, are older and younger people who joined the church after the pastor's tenure commenced, or what he calls newberries.[16]

George's theory provides an excellent study and idea, but allow me to expand upon his concept. In the church, a new pastor will certainly discover those who were members or attenders before he arrived, and he will have people begin to join once he starts his pastoral service. The power struggles and bases are unfortunately true. Battles over power are not one of those topics that we like to address or even admit in the church. We like to think of ourselves as being above this secular mind-set, yet a simple study of Scripture will demonstrate why the church faces such problems.

Genesis 3 unveils to us how sin entered the world. Eve ate the fruit from the tree of the knowledge of good and evil, and she gave some to Adam and he also ate. When God came to fellowship with them in the garden during the cool of the day, He confronted Adam over what he had done, and the first power struggle was born. When God inquired how Adam knew that he was naked, He asked, "Who told you that you were naked? Did you eat from the tree that I commanded you not to eat from?" (Gen. 3:11). Adam's response is classic: "The woman You gave to be with me—she gave me some fruit from the tree, and I ate" (Gen. 3:12). The initial thought occurs that Adam blamed Eve for the fact of his sin, a statement that clearly demonstrates the first battle for power within the family. The ultimate blame was placed by Adam upon God. The woman *You* gave to be with me. Adam both ignored his own part in the volitional commitment to sin, but he also sought to use this devastating event as means to bring division to the community (albeit it was an incredibly small unit of faith!).

Fast-forward a few years. Cain and Abel presented offerings to the Lord. God accepted Abel's offering but He rejected Cain's. In his anger, Cain killed Abel and then denied any wrongdoing (Gen. 4:3–9). Within this sin, one discovers the makings of a power struggle that poured over into a murderous act. The denial of Cain, "Am I my brother's guardian?" (Gen. 4:9), clearly reveals the connection between sin, power, and personality. Put these things together and you have the makings for a church in decline.

What I have learned that the pastor will discover is that, within his church, five groups of people will be present. While most characteristics fit each grouping, exceptions do exist, especially among the ranks of those who are already members of the church.

The Thirties. The first group I identify as possible power brokers within the church are those who have been in the church for at least thirty years. It is why I call them my *Thirties.* Within this age grouping will be those who will probably be older than the pastor, but this faction will also include those who are younger.

THE OLDER THIRTIES. The makeup of the older group, as it actually is in all of the groups, will be diverse. Some of the Thirties will have been in the church their entire lives. Their parents and even grandparents were members of the church. I pastored a church in Tennessee that had its beginnings in 1823. Many of the people in this church had roots from years gone by. They had been with the church through the good times but, more important, through the bad times. (As a side note, this phenomenon is quickly eroding, as people today are far more mobile.)

Some within the Older Thirties grouping may not have deep family roots in the congregation, but they have been in the church long enough to establish themselves in leadership. They teach the Sunday school classes, have been willing to work their way up through the committee structure until finally they have been asked to serve in key leadership positions, and they consider the church to be "their" church, as do most all of the Thirties.

Now enter this young pastor with visions of leading the church to mega-world status. He has all of the ideas, the vision, and the passion. He expects that the Thirties will follow him because, after all, he is the pastor. From this scenario, it becomes easy to understand why pastors have such short tenures, especially in churches in need of revitalization. To understand how to work with this group of people, one must understand their perspectives.

- They were in the church before the pastor arrived, and they will be there after he leaves. In other words, they have stuck it out through thick and thin.
- They are financially invested in the church. Most probably, all of the buildings were built and paid for by these people. In many cases, the buildings were originally built by family members now deceased. An incredible amount of nostalgia is involved at this point.
- They have heard it all before. This new pastor is not the first one to come along with great ideas. They also know that he probably will not stay long, especially if he is young and/or is working on an advanced degree.
- They have waited their turn to lead and are not willing to give that leadership (or power) to anyone. This fact is especially true

in churches where "man worship" is very prominent. "Man worship" occurs when church members exalt certain individuals as either pillars or spiritual giants. This "worship" drives egos very well.

- They have their system of friends and their circle of influencers long established over many years. This system can be positive because it demonstrates how the church has cared for its members through the years.

- They have grown accustomed to the church facilities. Therefore, updates, new technology, and even high-maintenance cleaning are not issues for them. On the other hand, because they have made the financial and personal investment in the building, they may view the building as "their" building. Thus, they do not want outsiders to be too visible or changes to be made to the facilities.

- In carnality, this group has few actual friends in the church but has learned which partnerships are needed in order to accomplish certain tasks or goals. There may be no honor among thieves, but power groups know the alliances that are necessary and are willing to enter those collaborations in order to get their way.

Two sad developments result out of these relationships. First, the pastor learns how to accommodate this group or the key individuals in order to accomplish his agenda. Sometimes he partners in the sinful behavior of power and compromise, knowing that he intends to move on to the next bigger church that comes his way. The second sad situation occurs when the new pastor decides that this group represents the enemy and determines to go against them and to break their power control. In some cases, the pastor might win. In most battles, he will be the loser. No wonder fifteen hundred pastors drop out of the ministry every month! The church is killing us and we are killing us.

Please understand that within this group of Older Thirties are people who have a strong investment in the church but also maintain a very balanced approach to ministry, leadership, and pastoral authority. *Not all Thirties are negative or critics.* Some have chosen to be the friend of the pastor and will be that confidant if the new pastor will develop a level of trust with them.

New pastors, and especially young pastors, make two mistakes in arriving at a fresh ministry opportunity. First, they are driven so much by passion that it overflows into running over people. I call it "arriving with both guns ablazin'." A problem occurs because, in the desire to get God's vision accomplished, some innocent people get hit along the way. The second mistake occurs when the new pastor assumes that change is needed just for the sake of change. If the church is in decline, it must mean that everything needs to be changed. Most of the time, things need to change, but when care is not taken in managing change, conflict arises. The pastor and the church get frustrated, and then the next scene depicts a firing or a resignation.

A pastor must be disciplined in order to understand these Thirties and to learn how to work with them, not against them. Here are a few suggestions:

- Make personal visits with each of the primary leaders of the church immediately upon arriving at the church. These visits may take some time; invest in making them. The pastor has heard from the search committee. He may have attended meetings where different individuals expressed opinions or desires. A personal visit allows the pastor to say that the opinion of a leader is important. It also says that he has the desire to listen, not just talk. Especially include in these visits the deacons and/or elders of the church. Find out who represents best the Older Thirties and visit them.

- In these visits, ask each individual to articulate, if possible, their personal vision for the church. The pastor might be surprised to discover that the vision he believes is right for the church is already shared by those who know the church better than anyone else.

- When possible, work to implement some of these vision ideas. Many times, the ideas of church members are simple tweaks of current programs or ministries. When people see that you are willing to listen and to be "their" pastor, they will be open to follow. The final section of this book addresses the issue of how to bring change about in the established church. Many of these processes will apply directly to the Older Thirties.

THE YOUNGER THIRTIES. This cross-section of people within the church is made up of those who have grown up in the church and, most probably, have spent their entire lives in one church. While the Older Thirties could quite possibly have church experience in other church contexts, the *Youngers* have very little knowledge of other churches outside of this one congregation. That fact alone makes it difficult in leading the Youngers. In fact, the pastor might discover that this particular group will be the most resistant to change, because the church under its old or current system impacted their lives and they do not want to see an end to that life. They especially want their children to experience what they experienced, and they resist anything that might be different.

This idea holds true in a number of areas. The Youngers might be resistant to the new pastor because he followed a long-tenured individual who baptized and performed the weddings for these Youngers. They might not even realize the extent of their rebellion against new leadership. This perspective also extends to certain programs and ministries. For example, many Christians remember the days of the youth choirs that wore fancy outfits and traveled the country doing choir concerts. Sometimes these concerts were billed as mission trips, but they involved primarily the use of a choir. Back in the early 1970s, musicals were written and published specifically for youth choirs. At the time for many churches, youth choirs were an effective way to get students involved in the church and even to reach out to some unchurched young people. Many people had their lives affected, some even changed, by these choirs. These individuals remember the importance this ministry played in their spiritual development, and they want that impact to continue. Thus, they ignore current trends and successful methodologies within student ministry. To even think of doing something different not only smacks at their nostalgia, it might even be interpreted as being near heresy. One can apply this logic to church camps, bus ministries, and day cares, just to name a few other obstacles.

Because their financial participation amounts to much less than their parents, the commitment level develops far more out of experience than is does substantive investment. They are now just beginning to be in positions of giving and can use their "tithes and offerings" as collateral for getting their voices heard. Yet, at the same time, they are a group with whom one needs to reckon.

Another characteristic with the Younger Thirties stems from the fact that they have been "waiting in the wings" for their turn at leadership. They have watched as their parents and others whom they admire have led the church, and they want their turn at this level of decision-making. Part of the problem they face is two-fold. First, they may not fully understand the commitment to leadership given by their predecessors. In other words, the definition and implementation of leadership by these Youngers might be totally different than the reality of leadership provided by the Olders. Second, because of "man worship," their motives might be off-center to some point. The Olders have led but with an integrity not recognized by the Youngers. The Olders led through the tough times of war and depression. They had to make the tough decisions regarding paying the light bill or paying the preacher. Faith played a primary role in their leadership. Because of these facts, they have been held in high esteem. The Youngers do not understand the cost of leadership. They are drawn to the notoriety and the power. Therefore, they are willing to make whatever compromises they need to make and to enter into whatever coalitions they need in order to secure their spot on the leadership teams.

This discussion obviously paints a very ugly picture, but one must return to Genesis 3 and 4 to understand how human depravity and the continued struggles that even Christians face with the flesh affect the church. The following offers a few suggestions for gaining the trust of Youngers:

- Build relationships with them by seeking ways to spend time with them. Let them see that you are not a threat to them.
- Build relationships with their children. Let the Youngers see that you are willing to pastor their children, just as they experienced ministry during their formative years in the church.
- Invite them to your home. One of the difficult aspects of ministry is balancing friendship with leadership. Researching this particular subject will yield a variety of conclusions, yet a clarity exists that says the pastor must develop a balance between these two ideas.

- Seek ways to attend and participate in their activities. The school PTA, sporting events, and concerts are some ideas available. Oftentimes, pastors arrive at a church and view their role as being purely spiritual and fail to invest in the lives of their members. This balance is also a difficult one.
- Be available to counsel them and make sure that you counsel them through God's Word. The young pastor gets into trouble when he thinks he knows everything about parenting, even though he has never been a parent or has only a toddler in his house. Youngers need their pastor to be available to help them work through biblical command and principle that makes sense.
- Do group mentoring and Bible study. Sometimes the church only sees the pastor preaching to the entire congregation. They never really have the opportunity to asks questions or to hear his heart. Youngers are drawn to small groups, so lead one that is open to anyone who wants to attend.

Remember that the Youngers are not the enemy either. Their ideas might be held captive by their generational experiences, but they have potential. This fact would be especially true for a church in decline. Probably few Youngers remain at this point, so their involvement is critical to the future of the church. Getting to know these Youngers might reveal that they also possess a vision for the church to survive and thrive. They have stayed because they have not given up on the church, yet change remains difficult for them. They fear, as do the Olders, that any changes instituted might spell the end of the church. They are "holding on for dear life." Resisting change means, in their minds, that maybe the decline will end. All of us know that an idea like that one most probably spells doom, but one can understand their dilemma. Additionally, the pastor, if things do not go well, can "believe that it is God's will to accept this bigger church that pays more money and is not in decline." Both the Youngers and the Olders know that possibility. They have probably seen it before. Therefore, do not give up on them. Some of the reasons for their staying with the church might be very selfish but other motives are nobler. Gain their confidence, and this assurance provides a huge advantage for the future revitalization process.

The Tens. A group that I have not discovered being discussed within the context of the stakeholders symmetry involves those who precede the pastor in tenure but have only been in the church for ten or so years. This group of individuals wields influence in the church, sometimes significantly, yet they hold a different perspective than do the Thirties. Here are some identifying marks of the *Tens*:

- They did not grow up in this particular church, therefore their viewpoints on ministry and vision have been developed through a totally separate set of circumstances.

- They obviously have remained in the church because they believe in her mission, at least to some extent to where they have not yet left to go to a vibrant, growing congregation in another part of town.

- They have been impacted by this church, as perhaps have their children. They are grateful for this church's ministry and still have a desire to support it.

- They were not overly connected to the previous pastor, even if he had a long tenure. He was the Thirties' pastor or he was just "passing through." The new pastor has a real chance of becoming their pastor. In the case of the established pastor, these Tens appreciate the fact that he has not "bailed out" on the church or was willing to accept the call of the church in spite of the challenges.

- Many of them have earned their way into leadership positions. In fact, many of those on the Pastor Search Team may be Tens instead of Thirties. As mentioned earlier, the risk of losing clout becomes great in decisions such as presenting the next pastor to the church. Many Thirties would rather influence behind the scenes in situations like searching for a new pastor. It is why the Tens will be more apt to accept the new pastor instead of the Thirties.

- Some of them may be waiting for a new pastor to arrive with a new vision because, though they are in some areas of leadership, they are not really allowed to lead. A new pastor might bring in a new vision that includes them. This fact is especially true in church leadership models that involve deacons and lay elders in decision-making processes. A Ten might be elected as a deacon, but his ability to lead is kept on a tight leash.

- The Tens will usually be, outside of the *Newbies* to be mentioned in a moment, the greatest supporter of the pastor if trouble ensues. Because of their positions, they offer more help and direction than do the Newbies. They have observed abuses, perhaps even in this very church, and do not wish to see their current pastor go through the same difficulties. Therefore, they stand with him.

In my opinion, some of the greatest influencers in the church will be the Tens. They have earned the trust of others, but they are not as resistant to change. It does not mean that some of them may act more like the Thirties than their peers, but the Tens may have the opportunity to make a great impact, especially on the Younger Thirties. A great deal of difference does not exist between Older Tens and Younger Tens because their terms of membership are so similar. The one exception will be with those Tens who were teenagers upon arriving at the church. Though they are now in their twenties, even some in their late twenties, they may not have achieved genuine leadership status. The good news is that these twenty-somethings offer a real resource for future leadership and ministry.

The Newbies. The final group of church investors is made up of those individuals who have joined the church or will join the church after the arrival of the present pastor. This dynamic is difficult to define because one would immediately believe that the reason these new people came to the church was directly associated with the pastor. What many stats demonstrate is that people do not initially attend a church because of the pastor, but the pastor significantly influences why they will return for a second visit and will eventually join a church. Compare the results of George Gallup with the conclusions drawn by researcher Thom Rainer. Though somewhat antiquated as research goes, these stats published by Gallup have actually remained steady for decades. The research is also pertinent because it relates well with the methodologies and programs of the established church, but it is clearly out of date when applied to church plants or most mega-church models. Rainer's research sheds light on the additional perspectives that influence these Newbies.

Gallup:

1. Came because of the Sunday school: 3 to 6%
2. Walked in of their own initiative: 3 to 8%
3. Came because of a particular minister: 10 to 20%
4. Came because of an evangelistic program: 10 to 20%
5. Came at the invitation of a friend or relative: 60 to 80%.[17]

Rainer:

1. 90%—Pastor/Preaching
2. 88%—Doctrines
3. 49%—Friendliness of Members
4. 42%—Other Issues
5. 41%—Someone at Church Witnessed to Me
6. 38%—Family Member
7. 37%—Sensed God's Presence/Atmosphere of Church
8. 25%—Relationship Other than Family Member
9. 25%—Sunday School Class
10. 25%—Children's/Youth Ministry
11. 12%—Other Groups/Ministries
12. 11%—Worship Style/Music
13. 7%—Location[18]

From these research findings, two conclusions can be reached regarding the Newbies and how they will connect with their pastor. First, they were probably invited to attend the church by a present church member. Therefore, do not assume that they will be totally loyal to the present pastor and to his vision. They will be influenced by that person or those groups who, not only invited them to attend a worship service, but now are connected to them through some ministry or small group. If those influencers are anti-change Thirties or Tens, then they may have a negative effect on these Newbies, thereby nullifying any participation in future vision and change.

Second, since they may have visited a second time because of the pastor's preaching, it behooves the preacher to develop skills that will enhance the ability to cast vision. It demands that pastors are committed to biblical preaching. Sermons, especially in the established church, serve a far greater purpose than just a means of passing time. This admonishment does not assume that everyone in the established church possesses a great passion for biblical preaching, but it demonstrates the fact that God's Word still changes people's lives and that preaching plays a significant role in casting vision.

Carl George concludes that these Newbies, and specifically what he identifies as junior newberries, will be the easiest people to lead and will be the ones who most easily follow the leadership of their pastor. The senior newberries, or those older than the pastor who joined after his tenure began, may be more reluctant to buy into the pastor's vision.[19]

In spite of these possible obstacles with the Newbies, they offer some extremely important value to the future of church revitalization. Note these characteristics:

- Because they are new, they will occupy little or no leadership positions in the church. Their level of influence will occur through giving and service. They will be the ones to accept the less desirable ministry positions, looking to "earn" their way into greater leadership opportunities.
- Their newness brings a potential freshness to the church. They may have joined the church out of a sense of mission. Many Newbies will have been members of other churches. They will bring with them ideas relating to vision, ministry, and potential.
- Many Newbies will be new converts, a fact that adds a great deal of excitement and potential for the future of the church. New believers know nonbelievers. They most probably do not have any church traditions that they hold sacred. They also will be most likely very loyal to the pastor and staff. If critics attack the pastor, these Newbies will be the first to defend their pastor.
- If the community is made up of older homes, *Older Newbies* will most probably be longtime residents of the neighborhood, though they were not, until now, members of your church. Some will actually be moving back to the community of their youth in order to retire. This fact gives them a sense of mission to ensure the future of their new church. They may have even been members during their teenage or young adult years.

- The Younger Newbies may have moved into the neighborhood because housing was more affordable. The house they purchased may be their first home. As a result, they probably will be more transient, living only a few years in their current house before moving to a newer or larger home in another community.

- Newbies could possibly be a source of threat for the Tens and especially the Thirties. If they come into the church with new ideas and desires, they may be rejected by the Thirties. This tragedy then makes it difficult to continue with any momentum. In most cases involving declining churches, new members and baptisms are more of the exception than the rule. If circumstances exist or occur that discourage new members, the process and time frame for revitalization becomes much more difficult and extended.

- Newbies may also create a sense of contention within the church because they are more likely to be the ones who create or desire ministries that demand finances that will primarily be provided by the Thirties. The Thirties may resent the Newbies for spending all the money and tearing up the facilities with their kids and programs.

- Generally, because of the reasons that led to decline, the church has to experience some level of revitalization before any new members can be reached. If the church has lost its desire to grow or if it has lost its reputation in the community due to conflict or lack of ministry, this need for initial revitalization becomes even more important.

Investors from the Community at Large

The second group of stakeholders in the church are actually people who do not attend the church. They are made up of the neighborhood, the surrounding community, and the city in which the church is located. The decisions that the church makes regarding ministry, building upkeep, property improvements or acquisitions, facility use, and even moral stances all play into the perspective that the community at large develops about the church. This idea being said, it behooves the church to think about, not only itself in decision-making, but also the impact that these choices will make in the surrounding area. One of the evidences that the church has lost its influence comes in the way that people respond to the decisions, changes, and improvements the church makes. The church no longer receives an automatic pass. The community scrutinizes every decision.

From churches causing property damage from the runoff of expanded parking lots, to local governments refusing property improvements or purchases, to possible lawsuits for standing for biblical marriage, to the person who criticizes the church because of the traffic clutter after Sunday service, the community at large plays an important role in church revitalization. If the church develops the reputation of running over or not caring about the community, the community will respond appropriately with criticism and rejection when the church seeks to finally reach out to its neighbors. Do not underestimate the importance of these investors. They comprise the group of the very people the church needs to reach, and if they have been turned off by any inconsiderate or uncaring attitudes of the church, the chances of reaching them and changing their minds will be slim.

Investors from the Invisible World

The discussion of the spiritual aspect of church revitalization has already been mentioned at length in earlier sections of this book. The revitalization pastor must not misjudge the spiritual realm of the church. It is easy to get focused on programs, methods, and the physical aspects of the church and forget about the spiritual. A fatal flaw that pastors make is to major on the physical and only give the occasional glance at the spiritual. While the church does not need to see a demon under every bush, recognize that much of the opposition the church faces is far more spiritual than it is material. Paul says,

> For our battle is not against flesh and blood, but against the rulers, against the authorities, against the world powers of this darkness, against the spiritual forces of evil in the heavens. This is why you must take up the full armor of God, so that you may be able to resist in the evil day, and having prepared everything, to take your stand. (Eph. 6:12–13)

Additionally, he reminds us that "the god of this age has blinded the minds of the unbelievers so they cannot see the light of the gospel of the glory of Christ, who is the image of God" (2 Cor. 4:4). Satan obviously does not want the church to succeed. In the spiritual realm of life, each church that dies represents one less voice in this lost world. Before and during revitalization, the church must remain aware of the spiritual part of renewal.

Conclusion

Over the next several chapters, eleven different reasons are going to be examined as to why churches fall into decline. I am confident that the process given to resolve the reasons for plateaued and dying churches, bringing about biblical change, and initializing revitalization will work regardless of the problem. Moreover, the fact that the problem is identified wins half the battle.

If some doubt still exists as to the absolute necessity for church revitalization and for pastors to commit themselves to this important ministry, take note of these additional overwhelming stats:

1. Very few of the 350,000 American churches are actually growing, mostly within the under 200 range or the over 2,000 range. The vast number in the middle is in decline.
2. Churchgoers are getting older and especially when compared to the general population. Millennials are, on the most part, unassociated with a local church.
3. Church attendance continues to decline. Forty percent of Americans say that they attend church. The actual number is probably closer to 20%.
4. From 2005 to 2010, the percentage of churches characterized by the phrase "high spiritual vitality" dropped from 43% to 28%.
5. Church contributions continue to drop on average. About 31% of congregations exhibited good financial health in 2000. That number dropped to 14% in 2010.
6. The percentage of teenagers who attend church has dropped from 20% to 15% in the last five years.
7. Every year, about 2.7 million church members become inactive.

8. From 1990 to 2000, church membership in Protestant churches declined 9.5% or around 5 million people. During that same period, the US population increased by 11% or 24 million people.
9. Half of all churches in America did not add any new members between 2010 and 2012.[20]

Each of the following chapters, along with the information included in this current chapter, will provide the necessary information in order for a pastor to do some effective assessment regarding the state of his current or potential church. Much of the assessment must be done through personal conversations and evaluations. Follow the ideas presented through these chapters as a foundation for making these assessments. The potential remains strong. The challenges are unlike in any other ministry or opportunity. Revitalization definitely demands a specific calling. The church obviously is losing ground in reaching the world, so a part of the answer to get the church back on track with God's mission is for pastors to help churches get back on track with God's mission. That is church revitalization!

CHAPTER

3

The Church Does Not Recognize the Need for Revitalization

When I first began teaching *Introduction to Church Revitalization* at Southern Seminary, I only included ten initial reasons that churches are in need of revitalization. In order to gain greater understanding into this dilemma and to research how others were handling this problem, I began meeting with different pastors and denominational leaders to gain insight from their experience and wisdom. Furthermore, I wanted to assist my students in connecting with churches that needed revitalization and were interested in having a pastor to lead them through such a process.

One of the people with whom I met serves the state organization for his denomination. Most of the students I teach are part of the Southern Baptist Convention, so it was important to meet with this leader in the Kentucky Baptist Convention. I explained that a part of my purpose was to connect churches with students. My interests also were in offering additional training that would be specific to Kentucky Baptists or any other state convention with which I was working.

Interest was expressed in establishing this type of partnership, yet I found his next statement to be intriguing. He said that, while he would desire to help in connecting churches with trained pastors, the biggest problem he faces in leading revitalization arises from the fact that the churches that need it rarely contact him for help, even though one of the areas of his job with the state convention is church revitalization. In other words, one of the obstacles to church revitalization grows out of the issue that these churches do not know that they need it. They are dying or, at best, are plateaued; yet they do not believe that either of those statements define their church. This situation occurs primarily in two church arenas.

The Suburban Church

The first set of churches that might not recognize their own demise will be medium-sized to larger churches in a suburban setting. These churches differ greatly from the downtown or urban church that can easily recognize the identifiable evidences of decline. They remember back to the days of old when the building overflowed with people and the pipe organ reverberated with joyous sounds of praise. Now, the pipe organ is rarely used and the sanctuary echoes more because of emptiness than mere acoustics. On occasion, they still may reside in a state of denial, but the evidence remains clear. All they have to do is look around, and they know that their church is dying.

The suburban church demonstrates much more subtle evidences. The rate of decline has been slow, thus not as visible as in other churches. If the question was asked, "Are you growing?" the response would be a resounding "Yes!" The facts would prove otherwise. Many suburban churches enjoy a significant enough number of new members who join from other churches and biological baptisms that somewhat mask for lay leadership the church's plateau or decline. This fact becomes especially true for the Thirties. In suburbia, particularly if no significant demographic change has occurred, transitional flight is less dramatic. The church will lose members due to death and job transfer, but the Thirties may not notice any real decline. Exasperating this idea is the detail that real church growth is not just identified through numbers but through church health. As stated before, many churches exist that exhibit growth in numbers but are genuinely unhealthy as New Testament congregations. The suburban church, frequently, fulfills this description. Consequently, church leaders do not recognize that they are in need of revitalization. Couple these ideas with the fact that most of the same people, the ones with whom the Thirties have established friendships, continue to attend and serve, and the resulting opinion remains that the church is doing well.

In all truthfulness, though, the church is not doing well. If the leadership would examine the church statistics over the past decade, they probably will find that, at best, the church has plateaued. In many cases, the church has actually experienced a small decline in numbers. Because of a general increase in salaries over the years, the budget numbers have grown but the actual number of givers has slightly declined. The leadership base remains the same because the same people who stepped into leadership ten years ago still occupy the same spots or have exchanged them within the stakeholders group. This type of church represents the kind of congregation that has a high resistance to change. Change expresses a negative conclusion because it may mean the end to the current group's power. New people represent a threat to this hierarchy, therefore evangelism and outreach hold positions that receive strong vocal affirmation but little actual involvement. In other words, *we do not want anyone to think that we are against winning people to Christ, but we really do not want these new people in our church because they might take our positions.*

As a result of these issues and others, the suburban, plateaued church may reject or resist any attempt by the pastor to bring about change, at least change in the areas that the Thirties deem important. These areas could be a detriment to the church or an outright reason for the church's decline, but those reasons are moot since no recognition exists to the church's slow demise. In fact, leadership may be in a state of total denial, a fact that could lead to even greater division and dissension. Questions will develop that ask why the pastor is trying to split the church. Meetings will become more contentious. The "us versus them" mentality that exists so prominently in many congregations will cancerously grow. All of these issues now create an atmosphere hostile to change and revitalization. The pastor leaves and a new pastor arrives who discovers that no discussion is allowed regarding these particulars. If he challenges present leadership structures, his tenure will be short-lived. If revitalization is going to happen, it will definitely be an extremely slow process. The pastor has to be willing to invest, not only the time, but also the patience to endure through the trials of change. In my opinion, this church represents the most difficult to help get on track to being a Great Commission church.

The Rural Church

The second church that oftentimes refuses to recognize the need for revitalization is the rural church, or what many call the country church. One cannot put these churches in a cookie-cutter category. In fact, these churches offer an incredibly interesting perspective and history.

The Rural Church That Is Now Surrounded by Development

With the expansion of cities and the flight of people out of metropolitan areas, many rural churches are finding themselves surrounded by new development. This trend has slowed somewhat since the turn of the New Millennium and especially with the crash of the economy in 2008. Yet there are those churches that find themselves trying to exist as the old country church established back in the 1800s, while all around them new families pour in. The Thirties represent the leadership of the church—the presence of two or three families who have a long history in the congregation and essentially run the church further complicates this problem. They not only have tenure, they have name dominance represented by the church patriarch and/or matriarch. The church has become their domain, and no one will be allowed to knock them off their tower. Their mantra is, *"We ain't changing."*

Let me give you an example. A young student was called to a local church that is visible from a major highway in between a large city and a medium-sized town. Subdivisions have been springing up around the church for years. None have been developed exactly in the church's back door, but the growth remains evident. The new pastor arrives with an enthusiasm to be able to grow this stagnant church by reaching young families. The church building has been the same for decades. Therefore, one of the first things that the pastor wants to do is to update the nursery. Someone in the church shares his vision and donates money to bring about the revitalization of this strategic children's area.

In the meantime, the "powers that be" do not agree with this strategy. The pastor makes the plans and looks to begin the process of initializing the updates. He approaches the church treasurer about releasing the money, only to be informed that, since the Thirties do not think that the nursery needs updating, they decided to give the money to missions. The money no longer exists for renovating the nursery. When the pastor confronts this man about this decision, he is told, "If someone does not want to come to our church because they do not like our nursery, then we do not need them anyway." The Thirties win and the pastor resigns discouraged. This scene can be reproduced multiple times a year.

Herein lies the problem. This church, and many others like it, does not believe that change or revitalization is needed. The same people remain in charge and are myopic to their own demise. Like the suburban church, no real significant numerical decline has been recorded. Many of these churches represent stagnation more than they do decline. Yet, at the same time, they do not recognize that their eventual destiny is death. New churches and new church campuses will spring up around them to reach those who can be reached. Churches like this one will fall into obscurity. They will be counted among the hundred thousand churches Rainer predicts to close their doors in the next decade. Sadly, at that point, it will be too late. It is like people who deny that they are sick, but upon going to the doctor and discovering the extent of their disease, demand that something be done immediately. They are still in denial even up to the point of death.

The Rural Church Still Located in the Country

In one medium-sized town where I served, a primary, country road extended from a major highway all the way into the next state. Although outside traffic rarely used this thoroughfare, it was well-known among the locals. As one traveled southeast toward the state line, several churches that cooperated within the same denomination dotted the landscape. About every five miles, either on the left or the right of the road, a small, red brick or white sideboard church building would be visible to the traveler. Each of these churches had around fifty people who attended services each Sunday. I often wondered what would happen if they got together and merged into one congregation. They would stop doubling up on several expenses, thus multiplying their available funds for other ministries and projects. They could hire full-time staff, with pastors designated, equipped, and impassioned to minister to this particular demographic group. In some ways I hoped that they never would catch onto an idea like that one because they would become competitors rather than non-players.

I made the mistake of suggesting that idea to the local denominational worker who was directly connected with these churches. I only mentioned it once, as it was not well-received. Unfortunately, if anyone travels down this road to this day, these same churches dot the landscape and most have a slightly smaller attendance today than a decade ago.

Why the reaction? One would think that an idea that would encourage growth, ministry, and mission would be, not only acceptable, but enthusiastically considered. Part of the problem occurred because of my own ignorance. I did not understand the rural church. Certain logistical issues would need to be resolved such as: Where would the new church be located and in whose backyard, what would be done with the remaining church buildings, who would be the pastor and what would happen to the other pastors, and how would the new church operate in polity and procedure? I am not saying that the resolution would be simple, but I am convinced that those churches would have a greater future together than separate.

The difficulty in dealing with many rural churches comes from the fact that they have been located in the same general vicinity for their entire existence. Two or three families essentially run the church. To their defense, it has been these families that have financially supported the church, have staffed the Sunday school, and have stepped in when no other leadership was available. They have a vested interest in the church and in the facilities. Most probably, their families literally built the church building. To give it up or to change it, even for something bigger and better, would seem to be an act of treason against their relatives.

Another problem stems from the past reality whereby the church maintained its growth because, as the families had children and grandchildren, those descendants became the next generation of leaders. By now, several generations have passed. Unfortunately, the church leaders do not recognize how many of their teenagers eventually leave the church for greener pastures (again, no pun intended). People in today's world are far more mobile than previous generations. Every church needs to take into consideration that with the Internet, people can research colleges, jobs, locations, housing, and about anything else they need to discover in order to make a move. In talking with several small college presidents, this fact has become a reality for them, forcing them to take their schools to another level in housing, athletics, and amenities. If they do not adjust and change, they will die. Students nowadays do not have to attend a local college or university. They can go anywhere in the world, making competition very fierce.

The local church needs to wake up to this same dilemma. Unfortunately for the rural church, many of them wear blinders regarding the future. It is difficult to bring vision and passion to a church that has stayed the same, not just for the last decade, but for the last century. In fact, any suggestion of change may be received as a threat to the current way of life. Although their children no longer stay on the farm to work with their parents, opting instead to move somewhere else to work in a new career, many leaders in rural congregations refuse to recognize the need for revitalization. They are hurting but are in denial. It takes a very special calling to work with churches like these, but a necessary calling and commitment nonetheless.

Barriers Abound

Several difficulties exist in trying to bring revitalization to the church that does not recognize the need for change. The first comes from the fact that pastoral tenure proves to be an issue in both the suburban and the rural church in denial. This characteristic relates essentially to all of the problems and remaining situations also. In smaller churches, especially those that are bi-vocational, pastors usually do not last long. The bi-vocational pastor is the oxymoron of pastoral ministry because he works a full-time job and then pastors a church full-time. His salary from the church may be part-time, but he still prepares three sermons a week, visits the hospitals, and counsels his flock. Burnout and pulpit exchange are rapid because the bi-vocational pastor recognizes that he is not making much of an impact in his current congregation. Therefore, he takes the next available church.

The suburban church does not face as much as the bi-vocational issue, but these churches will also experience rapid turnover in pastoral tenure because they are hiring the young, up-and-coming pastor who is open to the next opportunity within the pastorate. He will not stay, especially if he faces opposition, because other churches are always looking for the next young pastor to lead them.

In order to initiate change within churches like these, the pastor has to be committed to stay. This fact stands true in every situation, by the way. Long-tenured pastors are rare because of the battles that ensue within many congregations. Usually between years four to seven—the crisis years—the church considers if they want the pastor to remain, and the pastor reviews his own commitment to stay. This simple factor probably plays into why so many pastors leave by their fourth year. The first eighteen to thirty-six months serve as the honeymoon stage. After three years, the church decides if they want the pastor, and the pastor decides if he wants the church. The years represent crisis years because it will be during this tenure that problems surface, accusations arise, and the general disposition of both pastor and members becomes evident. Most people do not like conflict, therefore a simpler solution is to keep the résumé current and the contacts fresh.

The positive side of this scenario is that the pastor really does become the pastor after year seven. It can happen earlier, but sometimes some people will never see the new pastor as their pastor. Yet, if he is patient and enduring, change becomes a real possibility.

Second, the long-tenured pastor represents a barrier to revitalizing these types of churches. It is an interesting comparison. Not all long tenures are negative. Many of the great and growing churches in America have had a pastor serving for more than a decade. Many of the church starts that have reached mega-stage are still led by their founding pastor.

The problem surfaces when the long-tenured pastor experiences one of two things. First, he loses his dream. It may be that he had a dream for the first ten years of his service. Those dreams have been fulfilled or dashed, and he has not developed a new dream. Therefore, the church falls into stagnation because the pastor has plateaued himself.

Second, the long-tenured pastor becomes an obstacle to growth and revitalization when he becomes too much like the negative Thirties in his church. If a pastor stays long enough and performs enough funerals, he and his wife become the patriarch/matriarch of the congregation. Thus, they become the greatest hindrance to revitalization because change represents a criticism of his tenure. The church then falls into stagnation because even the leader will not lead.

Conclusion

Before an individual considers church ministry of any sort and church revitalization in particular, these issues need to be explored and contemplated. Any of us are subject to these temptations and to take our rest in a plateaued or declining church. These scenarios do not mean that these churches are incapable of growing or being healthy. They possess potential in that they have an established presence in the community, including the mid-sized to large suburban church. The rural church will battle the issue of power bases and residual reputation, but they will also have made an impact in the community through the varied ministries carried on by the church.

The difficulty in revitalizing churches like these surfaces from the idea that gives this chapter its title. They just do not recognize the fact that they need revitalization and change. Though extremely difficult, this obstacle does not present an impossibility. They can change.

CHAPTER

4

The Church Does Not Want to Grow

In my opinion, this reason provides the most significant and pertinent issue churches face today. While all of the remaining assessments play major roles in church decline, this reason, expressed in two dynamics, offers the most difficult problem to solve and the most complicated one to immediately assess (in most cases).

A Spiritual Issue

The bottom line of why churches and Christians reject the idea of biblical church growth remains a mystery; yet, for the entire time that I have served in ministry, reaching unbelievers, growing the church, and experiencing a genuine outpouring of God's Spirit have been fought, debated, and rejected. Sometimes the issues are actually spiritualized by saying that we do not need to put so much emphasis on numbers. Other times, genuine church revival scares people because it means that, not only does their neighbor need to get right with God, they themselves need to get right with God.

A definite spiritual deficiency attributes to the reason why many churches reject healthy growth. It is a spiritual issue. It starts with the pastor, moves to the paid and volunteer staff, and culminates in the life of the congregation. Understandably, people can point to past failures or especially past manipulative measures that were used under the guise of growing the church. Most Christians reject such shenanigans, but they do exist and have been done. We cannot, however, use the example of the impudent few as an excuse for allowing churches to die or for Christians to fall into stagnation. Please understand this one fact: *The problem of spiritual deficiency does not necessitate the rejection of the established church as unredeemable.*

I have heard people blame their generational characteristics. I have listened to individuals bemoan the concept of growth numbers as spiritually insignificant, only to talk about needing a raise, growing their business, and wanting a certain number of children. Numbers can be just that: numbers. They, in and of themselves, can be incredibly unspiritual. We can make numbers say whatever we want them to say, and we can use them as the sole reason for our existence, even in the church. Those problems do exist and often the established church rejects the idea of growth and health because of them.

The spiritual issue remains, nevertheless. Why would we not want the church to reach those who do not know Christ and those who are in need of spiritual growth to the point that it reflects in our attendance? Big is not always better, but death is worse. To the pastor who goes into the church that has been stagnant or in decline for years, be aware. They may have stated specifically that they want to grow, but the fact remains that they may not really want to grow, especially if that growth demands a price.

Assessing the spiritual condition of a church offers one of the most difficult challenges to determine and even more to repair. If the church does not want to grow and the reason lies in the lack of spiritual growth in the church, the pastor needs to set aside most any major plans or vision and concentrate on developing disciples.

At this point, my advice would be to return to the admonition found in Ezekiel 37. The soldiers were dead, and their bones were dry. Did they know that they were dead? I would say, "Probably not." Death implies the inability to respond to outside stimuli. These soldiers perhaps knew that they were dying, but now that death has come, the remaining body just lies there and decays. It does not know that it is dead and does not know what to do about it.

Think of it this way. In Luke 15, Jesus told three parables about the lost: the lost sheep, the lost coin, and the lost son. (Although I would agree with many scholars who say that the real emphasis of the three is on the seeking and loving shepherd, woman, and father, not the lost items or people.) In examining the three parables, they can be placed in three categories:

1. The lost sheep: those who are lost, know they are lost, but do not know what to do about it.
2. The lost coin: those who are lost, do not know they are lost, and therefore do not know what to do about it.
3. The lost son: those who are lost, know they are lost, and know what to do about it.

The church in need of revitalization that has fallen into spiritual decline probably falls into the second category. Their lostness represents not that they are spiritually unsaved but that they are spiritually out of touch with God. A coin, even when lost, still remains the possession of the person who owns it, even if that person does not know where the coin is located. I want to be careful here not to take the analogy beyond its intention by Christ because I do believe He is addressing spiritual lostness far more than relating the parable to those who know Him.

The spiritually dead church probably does not know that it is dead. The congregants, usually the Thirties, can live enough in the past that, as they remember when they fought valiantly for Christ, they can still think they are alive. They, however, are dead, do not know that they are dead, and really do not know what to do about it. The immediate reality is that change is not going to happen easily among those who do not know that they need to change. It is very much a spiritual issue, both in reality and in initiating change.

Dealing with Opposition

As Jesus walked on the face of this earth, He encountered numerous situations of opposition. Read the Gospel of John, and that fact becomes a stark reality. John 8 opens with the situation of the woman caught in adultery. A simple reading of the text reveals the depth of hypocrisy that permeated the lives of this theological group called Pharisees. They were deeply spiritual men in a sense, but it was a dead spirituality. They were dead but did not know that they were dead. Connect the dots of Ezekiel 37 and the words of Jesus in Matthew 23:27–28:

> "Woe to you, scribes and Pharisees, hypocrites! You are like whitewashed tombs, which appear beautiful on the outside, but inside are full of dead men's bones and every impurity. In the same way, on the outside you seem righteous to people, but inside you are full of hypocrisy and lawlessness."

This description defines this gathering of individuals, seeking to catch Jesus in a fault. They bring a woman caught supposedly in the act of adultery, a capital offense (though all of us recognize the sheer duplicity of this act because the adulterous man is nowhere to be found). Jesus forgives the woman and embarrasses her accusers. As a result, debate ensues concerning a variety of subjects. Finally, in John 8:48, they get to the subject of Abraham, actually accusing Jesus of being demon possessed because of His declaration that people will have eternal life if they keep His Word. Then, in the midst of the argument, Jesus declares, "I assure you: Before Abraham was, I am" (John 8:58). At that point, the Pharisees sought to stone Jesus because He equated Himself with God the Father, essentially declaring Himself as God. It would be throughout the ministry of Jesus that He faced opposition.

Even within His own ranks, resistance appeared. In Matthew 16, a passage referenced in an earlier chapter, Jesus commends Simon Peter for the extraordinary statement declaring the purpose of Christ and His subsequent use of that statement to speak of the hope for the church. Yet, in the midst of this jubilation as Jesus later describes the cost of the church's future, Simon Peter rebukes Jesus. And how did Jesus respond? He says, "Get behind Me, Satan! You are an offense to Me because you're not thinking about God's concerns, but man's" (Matt. 16:23).

Those words describe, unfortunately, the very situation that occurs in many declining churches. Christians express fear and foreboding with respect to growth and revitalization because they regard the concerns of humanity over the concerns of God. I do not believe that, in most cases, people possess an actual awareness of this problem, but it exists nonetheless, I have found that, when it comes to how Satan attacks the church today, he uses God's own people far more than he does those who are outside of the church. Satan did that in opposing Jesus.

So do not get upset, turn in a resignation letter, and call in every resource available to get a résumé posted when opposition raises its ugly head. Jesus faced opposition, as did the prophets of old and the pastor down the street. When opposition occurs, here are a few suggestions for how to handle it:

Do Not Ignore It

One of the mistakes pastors make in dealing with opposition is to follow the idea that, if it is ignored, it will go away. Unfortunately, it will not. One of the effective measures for dealing with opposition comes from the simple process of showing that you care what others think. I immediately recognize that this particular suggestion can backfire, as expressed by many and various writers on the church. For example, Gary McIntosh addresses the four groups of people that a pastor will normally engage in a church. One of those groups he calls the VDPs or the Very Draining People. He equates the group called the VIPs, the Very Important People, with the disciples. The VDPs he associates with the Pharisees and the Sadducees (two interesting designations). McIntosh explains:

> As you work to revitalize your church, you must decide where to invest your time. All four of these groups will want you to be with them. Revitalization pastors tend to spend time with the VDPs because they demand to be heard. However, revitalization leaders spend time with the VIPs and the VTPs (very trainable people), preferring to invest in those who will prove helpful in the process of revitalization.[21]

One can hardly fail to agree with McIntosh's assessment. If a pastor spends too much time with those that complain and drain, no investment is made in the lives of others. I would caution, however, totally ignoring these sort of people, especially if they rank in the Thirties category. Like Jesus, lead as a servant and with fearlessness, but if genuine revitalization remains the goal, one of the ways that the pastor can get the Thirties on board happens when real concern and listening result with those who express opposition to the pastor's vision. In other words, when opposition happens, you had better care about it because that opposition may be the one thing that keeps revitalization from taking place.

Think How the Opposition Thinks

In caring about opposition, do not be blind sided by those who may oppose the vision or the need. This fact becomes especially true when presenting ideas of change, growth, vision, or decision, especially in serving in an established church that conducts business meetings. Unfortunately, the business meeting setting serves as one of the secondary motivating factors behind church planting. Younger pastors want to plant churches so that, in their polity, business meetings do not take place. It also makes the elder model of leadership so attractive to many in ministry. Most decisions come through the leadership of elders rather than through the deacon or committee structure and resulting in the business meetings. Business meetings can become contentious and be a sounding board for the critic.

Remember this fact: Jesus always had an answer for His critics. I do not believe that He took them lightly. Because of Who He was, He knew the thoughts of people, but His example speaks clearly to us. In order to effectively handle opposing views, know ahead of time how they think, the questions they will ask, and the criticism they might express. In presenting a major idea, think through the questions and have prepared a FAQ sheet for those in attendance. This move demonstrates that those who are presenting this matter have thought through the process but have also listened to those who have expressed doubt. Sometimes that simple act silences the critics because all they want is a voice. The Thirties, especially the Older Thirties, become critics because, as they reach their senior years, it becomes apparent that no one is listening to them. They made the financial, personal, and congregational sacrifices to ensure the future of this church and now no one, including the Younger Thirties, is listening to them. So hear the critics and think how they think.

Find Someone Who Has Dealt with It

One of the best resources for church revitalization comes from those pastors who have done it. Pastors make a huge mistake when they fail to seek advice or input from others, especially those who have greater wisdom and experience in these particular matters. As important as it is for a prospective pastor to interview former pastors of the church in consideration, it is just as important for pastors to find others who can serve as a resource with regard to church revitalization or church problems. While all churches are unique, they are also the same. Do not be afraid to reach out to that pastor or layperson who may have insight into your particular decision-making process. Hebrews 12 admonishes Christians to press on in the Christian life, seeing that "we also have such a large cloud of witnesses surrounding us" (Heb. 12:1). Pastor, do not serve alone. Reach out to fellow pastors, denominational leaders, seminary professors, and godly laypersons and ask them for advice. The strutting rooster may end up as Sunday dinner if he is not careful. Find someone who has been through what you are facing and talk with them.

Talk with Some of the Key Opposition Leaders in Advance

Meeting with people in advance offers another way to help avoid confrontation and ungodly argument. While many of these steps may seem time consuming, and they are, their investment may produce some much-needed return in the future. As already mentioned, many times people stand in opposition to something because they do not believe that their voice is being heard. To their defense, pastors often become so focused on the vision and the need that they fail to see the people whom they serve. This fact becomes especially true with critics. No one likes critics or criticism, so one of the easiest ways to handle them is to run over them. Get on the train because it is leaving the station. If somebody gets in the way, run over them.

That idea works well in movies and reads well in books, but its practicality lacks greatly. If the pastor continues to run over the flock, soon no flock will remain. *Pastor, do not become myopic in vision-casting.* Remember, the vision serves the church, not vice versa. Therefore, in preparing for leading the church to embrace change and to revitalize, have the courage to talk with some people who may be opposed to this new direction. It could have the benefit of bringing them over to your side, but it at least lets people know that you are listening.

Be Ready to Answer Questions with Real Answers

In thinking how the opposition thinks, do not be offended when questions surface. Sometimes those in opposition can discourage others in a meeting and change their way of thinking or even their vote by the questions they ask. It is also true that some people do not know how to ask a question in a public forum. They become nervous, and their voices and vocal inflections imply anger rather than inquiry. Therefore, pastors have a tendency to try to quash questions, or they respond with curtness or with condescension. Neither of those responses demonstrates a Christlikeness or wisdom.

If an awareness surfaces of specific areas of opposition, be ready to respond to those questions with real answers. Sometimes believers resist growth because they are the ones that have to pay for it but never benefit from it. They end up supporting it but then are criticized when it fails. They have been burned in the past and do not wish to revisit the mistakes. Therefore, they meet any change with resistance, and this fact behooves the pastor to think ahead of time about questions that might be asked.

Know Your Strengths and Weaknesses

When dealing with opposition and in thinking like the opposition thinks, remember this important fact: *Those who may oppose the pastor's ideas are not the enemy.* Pastors often get focused on the personalities of the opposition rather than the issues and ideas of opposition. Therefore, they enter into a meeting unprepared for questions and answers.

An important step in assessment and presentation comes from preparation. Take a look at the proposal and then strategize regarding the strengths and the weaknesses of the presentation. A business model called SWOT essentially addresses this process. SWOT stands for:

Strengths

Weaknesses

Opportunities

Threats

From an assessment standpoint, a prospective pastor can evaluate the positive and negative challenges a particular church presents. This process demands that one think along these lines of appraisal as interviews are conducted. Questions relating to the very concepts of a willingness to grow and the cost of growth need to be asserted. The particular answers do not necessarily dictate the final decision in choosing to become a church's pastor, but they allow the pastor to be aware of the particulars of the challenges ahead.

In presenting change and the particulars of revitalization, this method becomes greatly advantageous. When those who hold opposing views due to past failures, short pastoral tenure, fear, or any other reason question the validity of a particular proposition, be ready to answer those objectives by having thought through these categories. If the church moves forward with this particular change, the following are the strengths, weaknesses, opportunities, and threats. A difficult dynamic in doing church lies in the fact that people want the church to trust God but to always have a plan B in place just in case God does not come through for them.

Faith offers an incredibly difficult concept to define and follow, especially in the physical world. Churches are quick to trust God in the abstract, but not so much in the concrete. Therefore, get the proper homework done when presenting changes that will move the church out of this level of complacency that says that they do not want to grow or are unwilling to pay the price for it. Additionally, little aids more in making other changes than having success in the early presentations.

Listen

This idea is not intended to be redundant or condescending. Several times already, the issue of listening has been mentioned. The reason for visiting this particular again is because most pastors with a passionate desire to see the church succeed will enter into negotiations and meetings with a set agenda and an unwavering focus. Unfortunately, when the dust settles, the church is left flustered simply because no one listened. When a listening ear is not prioritized, condescension becomes an easy response and ill-formed questions become an easy target. Therefore, listen; really listen to people. If people are not the enemy, then listen to them. It may be that their questions or comments are unfounded or even silly; but if the pastor takes time to listen to these inquiries, people will be more apt to follow the plan, even if they do not agree with it, than if their questions were ignored.

Keep Cool

Proverbs 15:1 says, "A gentle answer turns away anger, but a harsh word stirs up wrath." Keeping cool offers a very interesting perspective in pastoral ministry, especially for those passionate, "type A" pastors. As a pastor, do not ever lose the passion for ministry and for God, but learn to buffer that passion in responding to criticism, complaint, or question. From a servant leader perspective, people expect the pastor to lead with grace and compassion. The fact that they may not make the same demand on themselves or others provides an unsolvable contradiction, but that paradox is the world in which pastors live. The world possesses the same expectation. Back in 2004, Howard Dean, in his bid for the United States Presidency, got overly excited in response to his third place finish in Iowa. His actions were concluded not to be very presidential, and he dropped in the polls. This one gaffe cannot be blamed for his defeat, but it certainly played a part in how people viewed Dean, even people who shared his political views.

The church expects their pastor to be passionate but to be in control of this passion. When under attack, when questions fly that appear to be rooted in accusation rather than inquiry, or when someone just gets nasty, stay in control and turn away wrath with kindness. People expect that, when put on the spot, someone will react with anger or a raised voice. Stay in control, regardless of the situation or the statements. In doing so, the pastor gains a great deal of support, simply because the church sees a reproduction of the mind of Christ in their pastor's life. The Thirties will appreciate the fact that he models Christ. The Tens will respond positively because they recognize that they have a pastor they can follow. The Newbies will be drawn by both the spiritual response and the servant mind-set. Even if someone puts the pastor in a "no-win" situation, keep cool. Always stay in control.

Be Willing to Wait

For most any Christian, waiting must be one of the most, if not *the* most, difficult tasks assigned by God. Yet the world has come up with a slogan to define this attribute: "Good things happen to those who wait." This idea actually originates in Scripture.

Consider Abraham and Sarah. God made a phenomenal promise to Abraham in Genesis 12:1–2:

> The LORD said to Abram: "Go out from your land, your relatives, and your father's house to the land that I will show you. I will make you into a great nation, I will bless you, I will make your name great and you will be a blessing."

At this point in their marriage, Abraham and Sarah had no children. The Bible speaks clearly as to the fact that Sarah was barren, meaning not just that she had no children but that she could not have children. Kenneth Mathews explains:

> Sarai's condition explains the attention given to the women of Terah's family. Not only at this point does Sarai have no beginnings, she also has no continuation through a child. The message is thunderous: the woman is a "weak link," we would say, in the chain of blessing. Her barren state dominates the Abraham story since the divine promises involve a numerous host of progeny for Abram (12:2a; 15:4–5; 17:1–2; 18:10). Here "she had no children" (11:30) underscores at the start the need for God's help (17:17; 18:11–12; 21:1, 7; Rom. 4:19; Heb. 11:11). This redundancy in the text occurs only for Sarai's barrenness unlike Rebekah (25:21) and Rachel (29:31), where "barren" alone occurs.[22]

This detail gives insight into the depth of despair and need that both Abraham and Sarah faced. Abraham was seventy-five years old at the time of this promise, with Sarah following close behind at sixty-five. Had they been teenagers, even with the fact that people were still living well over one hundred years of age, people might not be as alarmed at these details. They were, however, reaching that point of being beyond childbearing years. If the promise was going to come, it had to be fulfilled quickly.

God, though, did not act quickly. In fact, it would be another twenty-five years before Sarah would give birth to Isaac, a miracle in itself considering that she was now ninety. God taught them the lesson to wait on Him. It would be the crisis that every leader of God's people would face in their times of leading, and it is the dilemma that each person in ministry faces, especially when change and revitalization are needed.

Learn from Scripture and make this application to your life and ministry. As pastors, we may be guilty of preaching the Word to our people and expecting them to follow the text. When it comes to our ministries, we struggle with those same admonitions. Sometimes, in God's timing in church revitalization, He tells us to wait. We want to initiate change quickly because we see the proverbial handwriting on the wall. We have done the assessments and demographic studies, and the results are not good. God, conversely, says, "Wait." It is one thing to miss God's activity; it is another to get ahead of God. Neither scenario produces fruit. Therefore, wait on God. If the timing is not quite right, then wait on God. He will tell you and the church when the time is right. To push ahead when the church emulates an attitude saying that it is not willing to pay the price to grow could be fatal, both for the pastor's ministry and the church itself. So as difficult as it is for all Christians, wait on God.

What to Do in the Meantime

When it becomes evident that opposition abounds and that the church as a whole is not ready to make the changes necessary to grow and to revitalize, it does not necessarily mean that it is time to resign. The pastor still has a prominent role in preparing the church for the next steps. These ideas permeate nearly every chapter of this book: preach, evangelize, pastor, and pray.

Preach the Word

We live in a time that it appears that preaching has lost its appeal or power, especially when the concept of proclamation enters the discussion. In many churches, preaching has been lethargic at best for years, and the people of the church have grown accustomed to sermons that neither teach nor challenge. In the established church, and in any church for that matter, the first step to leading the church back into a desire to grow can come through a systematic preaching of God's Word. This volume will not allow for a polemic or pedagogy to be presented on preaching, but what I would highly encourage anyone who desires to create a change in the growth climate of the church to do is to preach biblical sermons.

John Piper posits that true biblical preaching finds its definition in expository preaching:

> It is my contention that all true Christian preaching is expository preaching. Of course, if by an "expository" sermon is meant a verse-by-verse explanation of a lengthy passage of Scripture, then indeed it is only one possible way of preaching, but this would be a misuse of the word. Properly speaking, "exposition" has a much broader meaning. It refers to the content of the sermon (biblical truth) rather than its style (a running commentary). To expound Scripture is to bring out of the text what is there and expose it to view. . . . The size of the text is immaterial, so long as it is biblical.[23]

Take the church through the book of Acts and show them how God moved in the lives of churches all over the world. A great sermon series idea is called *Sailing through Uncharted Waters* that traces how often in Acts Christians were forced to do something that had never been attempted. Luke's historical account of the church's beginnings is replete with stories of success, failure, revival, and revitalization, even within the early years of the ecclesiastical movement. I am convinced that many pastors will be amazed at the change that occurs naturally and the opportunities that open for discussion once biblical preaching ensues. So preach the Word.

Practice Personal Evangelism

The church may have lost her vision, but do not get caught in the trap of doing only maintenance visitation or not visiting at all. Do not lock yourself up in the pastor's study, ready to share a word from God but not having spent time with God's people and with those who are outside of Christ. Practice personal evangelism and take someone with you from your church.

In many smaller communities and rural areas, door-to-door visiting still maintains much value. In larger cities, this type of visitation increasingly sees opposition in some regards. We read of the negative prognosticators who bewail all church visitations as the Pterodactyl of modern church ministry. And in some cases, they are correct. But while the pastor may not be able just to show up unannounced at someone's doorstep, doing personal evangelism can still be accomplished.

If some form of traditional visitation is out of the question, strategize on how personal contacts can be made. Start with the church membership roll. Be available to preach funerals through the local funeral home for those who do not have a pastor. Do so without charge, if necessary. Join the local Chamber of Commerce or service club. Through those contacts, look for ways to share the gospel with people who do not know Christ and take someone from your church with you if at all possible.

While the church may have lost its vision for evangelism and growth, that passion can be rekindled when Christians see people publicly professing their faith in Christ. If your area is somewhat hostile to the gospel or to personal visitation, look for ways to do acts of kindness or what is called servant evangelism.[24] When you have established those relationships, the door will open to share Christ, and when you have that opportunity, make sure that you take someone from your church with you (perhaps you are seeing a pattern here).

Changing the church's mind-set with regard to growth becomes difficult when past problems exist and resistance occurs, but when a believer sits in someone's living room or at the burger joint and watches as another person takes that step of faith whereby they move from spiritual death to life, a transformation occurs. It happens in the person who previously did not know Christ, but it also ensues in the life of the observing believer. At that point, the change takes place in the church one person at a time. As this revolution births, it expands and multiplies in the lives of others within the congregation. The process still may be slow, but the church changes one person at a time. Practice personal evangelism on a regular basis.

Pastor the People

Seeking to bring change into a church becomes a very demanding effort. To do nothing, in appearance, offers a much easier road. That level of apathy and complacency probably serves, from a pastoral standpoint, as to why many churches are stagnant and dying. Pastors just do not want to get into a fight trying to get the church to grow, so they draw a paycheck and keep their heads low.

When it appears that the only solution afforded at a particular time is to wait, do not lose heart or lose the opportunity to grow through the conflict and delay. Paul's advice to the Ephesian church should be heeded at this point:

> Let no one deceive you with empty arguments, for God's wrath is coming on the disobedient because of these things. Therefore, do not become their partners. For you were once darkness, but now you are light in the Lord. Walk as children of light—for the fruit of the light results in all goodness, righteousness, and truth—discerning what is pleasing to the Lord. Don't participate in the fruitless works of darkness, but instead expose them. For it is shameful even to mention what is done by them in secret. Everything exposed by the light is made clear, for what makes everything clear is light. Therefore it is said:
>
> Get up, sleeper, and rise up from the dead, and the Messiah will shine on you. Pay careful attention, then, to how you walk— not as unwise people but as wise—making the most of the time, because the days are evil. (Eph. 5:6–16)

Make the most of the time. When obstacles arise or when it seems that any process of change or revitalization will take eons of time, instead of sending out résumés and fretting over any lack of growth, spend time in personal spiritual formation and in being faithful to the tasks of the pastor. Evangelize, preach, teach, visit, and do ministry. Coupled with the temptation of doing nothing is the desire to hold up in the pastor's study surrounded by the books of those admirable and envied authors. If only this church was like these other churches. Instead, keep doing what the calling of God demands. Trust God that He will work in His timetable.

Remember also that these days are evil. Doing the Lord's work is often tedious and draining. The preaching event demands that one wrestle for the souls of men and women, thus becoming the most exhausting task of the pastor. Therefore, if the pastor does not commit to a systematic and current process of personal, spiritual growth, eventually emptiness and despair result. What only serves as a minor distraction becomes a major development and focus. The church fails to revitalize because the pastor lacks personal revival. So while waiting patiently on God, work and grow. Leave the résumé on the computer (or in the file cabinet).

Prioritize Congregational Prayer

This idea is detailed in chapter 13, so I will not belabor the point here. Yet, the one thing that the pastor needs to do when waiting on God is to pray. Practice personal prayer and devotion and lead the church to be a praying church. While it may be assumed that everyone will favor this activity, the unfortunate discovery may be that even prayer is resisted. Therefore, be patient in leading the church to pray. It may need to start small, but do not give up on what prayer can do. Remember the words of James, "The urgent request of a righteous person is very powerful in its effect" (James 5:16).

Conclusion

These first two areas of assessment, either that the church does not know that it needs revitalization or that it simply does not want to grow or pay the price to grow, provide the two most difficult issues both to assess and to repair. Sometimes the only hope that churches like these have is for God to move mightily. Every church needs to see a movement of God, but those churches in rebellion to or in denial of their demise need God most urgently. During these days, make sure that the prayers offered in the pastor's study reflect this desperation and demonstrate a faith that demands God's attention. God may not be moving because the church never attempts anything that requires His power nor offers any prayer that genuinely reflects this absolute dependence and need for Him. Jesus spoke of *vain repetitions* (Matt. 6:7 KJV) in the prayers of the Pharisees; so make sure that the prayers offered in the pastor's study do not reflect that level of praying. Be desperate. Be honest. Be faithful.

5 ✱ *entire chapter*

Physical Barriers to Growth

From the moment that a church begins, barriers will surface that offer real obstacles to that church going to the next level. A number of books have been published and chapters written that address growth barriers: the 200 barrier, the 800 barrier, the 1000 barrier, and so on. The church in need of revitalization is not focused on growth barriers because growth is not a present reality. What many church leaders fail to recognize, though, is that the plateaued church faces some real barriers to genuine turnaround. These barriers must be assessed and eliminated in order for the church to get on track once again. Then the church can address the growth barriers that will arise once the church experiences real revitalization, a problem that should be a welcomed challenge.

Facilities

One of the greatest hindrances to revitalization and getting the church back on a growth track is the church facilities. An easy assessment that both a prospective pastor and seasoned pastor can make comes from evaluating the condition, location, and use of the church property. When a church sits on a plateau or is in decline, the buildings and grounds turn out to be one of the first areas of neglect. Money becomes tight, and the church initiates a deferred maintenance program. Additionally, the longer an individual's membership exists, the less apt that person is to look at the church facilities with a critical eye. In fact, a protectionism can develop among the Thirties because they are the ones who built and maintained the buildings. A criticism of the facilities could be perceived as a personal attack on them. That fact alone demonstrates why the simple act of change becomes increasingly difficult. Buildings serve as a source for turf wars, thus care must be taken in initiating this level of change. Be careful not to drive people to fix their facilities. Lead them to make the changes. Chapter 14 addresses this process in detail.

Facilities Assessment

Observing the facilities offers a firsthand look at needs and areas of neglect. The following provides a checklist of questions and perceptions for assessing the condition of and positive/negative attributes of the church facilities.

What Is the Overall Condition of the Church Property?

When someone first drives up to the entrance of the church, what does that person see and encounter? When a church faces decline in numbers and revenues, the church grounds often fall into neglect. It could be that a church member has volunteered to take care of the grounds, but if that individual does not maintain particular principles of work and expectation, the neglect occurs more out of apathy than it does because of finances. Oftentimes, because volunteers are sometimes unappreciated, their work suffers. This fact is especially true in taking care of the church property. If the grass is not mowed and the bushes are not trimmed, this neglect communicates to the visitor that these people must not care about their church. In fact, this statement can be applied to each of these assessments, and it shows why attention and assessment must be given.

In addition to the grounds, what is the overall condition of the building exterior? Oftentimes, the church is in need of fresh paint or repairs to guttering and woodwork, along with a host of other problems. Again, these issues speak to the general feelings the church has about itself and the impression left on newcomers.

What Is the Condition of the Nursery and Children's Areas?

As mentioned in an earlier chapter, this issue provides a wealth of information concerning the thoughts of the church at large, but it also offers the opportunity for battles to ensue. Longtime church members may not care about the condition and the smell of the nursery, but newcomers, especially those with their first child, will care deeply. It is amazing how quickly this area can become rundown and can reek of unpleasant odors. Of all the areas of concern regarding facilities, this one probably serves as the top priority, especially if the church desires to reach young families.

In addition to the condition of these areas, examine the location of each. If the church facilities have multiple floors, are the children's/preschool areas on the first floor? Are they located near an exit? These factors also must be taken into consideration if the church runs some type of preschool/daycare throughout the week. Many churches ignore safety issues regarding children, especially if these programs have existed for some time. Church members and workers forget that times have significantly changed over the last couple of decades, especially in the realm of church safety. Take a look at how the church protects its children and what measures need to be implemented in order to enhance these safeguards.

What Do the Major Hallways Communicate?

Frequently, with older facilities, hallways are narrow, dimly lit, and in need of a face lift. These factors are true, not just for the areas rarely visited by people, but even in the places where the primary flow of traffic takes place. As in all of these scenarios, the church communicates a negative perspective about itself through a lack of attention to detail.

Geoff Surratt wrote an article for *ChurchLeaders.com* entitled "3 Not-So-Obvious Reasons Visitors DON'T Return to Your Church." One of the reasons he proffered was "Your church doesn't care about details." Surratt explained:

> During the service, the guest noticed that the words were wrong on some of the slides, and there were several typos in the bulletin. On they [sic] way out to the car, they noticed the pile of junk on a table in the corner, seemingly the same pile of junk that was

there when they visited last Christmas. In the parking lot, the overgrown flowerbeds seemed to emphasize the message, "We do the least we can." The new attender can't help but wonder why the church leaders care so little about details. Maybe that's the way they treat people as well?[25]

His words should be well taken and applied to every area of the church. If the hallways are crowded, people are bumping into each other, tables and other obstacles are blocking access, walls are unpainted, and floors are in lackluster condition, the church then communicates an unwelcoming perspective, whether intentional or unintentional.

What Does the Primary Church Sign Communicate?

In today's world, especially for churches located in larger city venues, rules and regulations oftentimes diminish a church's ability to advertise itself even on its own property. Over a period of time, churches begin to take for granted its signage, allowing these forms of communication to become outdated, to fall into disrepair, or just to become a general eyesore in the community. Oftentimes these factors indicate the financial distress of the church because sign upkeep is expensive and obviously not on the priority list. Additionally, everyone coming to the church knows the church's location and name, so what is so important about a sign?

When I was interviewing for my current church, I went across the street to the Walmart to buy something. As I was checking out, I asked the clerk if she knew where the church was located, naming the church by name. She responded, "I've never heard of that church." Literally, our church sits at a direct right angle from the Walmart, less than a thousand yards away, yet this individual had never heard of the church. Part of the problem stemmed from a marketing issue, but the other part developed from poor signage and visibility. The primary church sign sits at an angle facing southbound traffic. At the time that the church relocated to its current property, little traffic flowed northbound. No one seemed to take into consideration future growth and traffic patterns. The sign itself is dated and, in many ways, unattractive. Additionally, when the church was built, shrubs and small trees were planted in front of the building. Thirty years later the shrubs stood eight feet high and the trees became massive structures.

The church staff resolved part of the visibility issue by removing some of the trees, a fact that still draws the ire of some church members. The shrubs were also removed. The signage problem continues to exist because a local ordinance prevents the church from updating or changing the sign. Fresh paint and lettering help, but only to a certain extent. The sign, in the opinion of some, speaks volumes about what the church thinks of itself. Few people in the church, however, really take notice. The problem exemplifies what happens in so many churches, even ones that have a desire to grow and be healthy. The small details hinder the church.

How Visible Is the Church Property?

Oftentimes, charter members think strategically about location and visibility. Over the years, and probably over the decades, those strategies become outdated, forgotten, and overrun by change.

On my "bucket list" was the desire to preach at a church in East Tennessee named for my family. The Henard clan came to America in the late 1700s, with the earliest family record dating 1796. In 1946, a cousin of my grandfather gave land for a church to be built, along with the lumber needed for the building that was completed in 1947. He had actually developed homes in the area for the men arriving to work with the newly established Tennessee Valley Authority. The development was named Henardtown and the church, Henard's Chapel Baptist Church.

At great risk by the pastor, I received a long-awaited invitation to preach. Upon arriving, I immediately noticed several things. Nearly seventy years after the founding of the church, the entire area had dramatically changed. A four-lane highway had been built, bypassing the original church location. Although established on top of a hill overlooking the area, trees and underbrush had grown, blocking the church's visibility from the new highway. The church had done well in placing a sign on the main road, but hindrances still existed in finding the church. I took several wrong turns before eventually stumbling onto the church property.

To the church's credit, they had voted a short time back to relocate and had purchased several acres on the main thoroughfare that led into town. The new location will provide better access and room to grow. Their current situation, however, provides a picture into the typical dilemma in which many established churches find themselves. Loss of visibility becomes an extremely slow process. Growth of trees, changes in demographics, and adjustments in traffic patterns do not happen overnight. One can see how easy it would be for church members to lose sight of these changes or to become so accustomed to them that they fail to recognize the negative impact these things are having or could have on the church. Yet visibility offers one issue that churches must address and most probably can resolve. It also speaks to the members' opinions about growth, revitalization, and the future.

What Is the Condition of the Most Frequently Used Women's Restroom?

Men do not care so much, but do not overlook the ladies. Next to the smell in the nursery comes the condition of the women's restroom. This subject is not the most pleasant of which to speak, but it is essential in understanding and assessing the church's perspective about growth. Think of this problem in this manner: women probably make up the majority of most congregations. Take into consideration the number of women who attend without their husbands, the reality that women outlive men in most situations (meaning that widows well outnumber widowers), and the fact that single moms make up one of the largest unreached people groups in America. These stats should cause the church to recognize immediately the importance of the women's restroom.

The problem occurs because men run most churches. The lead pastors are men, as are the deacons. Men comprise most building committees, as well as being the primary hire for building superintendents or head custodians. Typically, men overlook the depth of what cleanliness should be, and that fact speaks volumes to newcomers, especially women.

What Is the Condition of the Worship Center?

All of the statements in the previous sections apply to the worship center. Longtime members overlook worn-out carpeting, poor sound systems, inadequate lighting, peeling ceilings, and broken pews. The Thirties know which pews are safe and which ones are not.

I remember from years ago a rural church that got into a huge fight over the condition of the facilities. The Tens wanted to build a new church. The Thirties believed that the current structure was adequate. If it was good enough for their grandparents, it was good enough for them. It was not until someone fell through the flooring in the sanctuary that action had to be taken. The county condemned the building as unsafe, forcing them to make a decision. Unfortunately, the church split. The Thirties purchased an old building a mile or so west of the original location and named themselves The Old Calvary Baptist Church. (The name is changed to protect the innocent and the guilty.) The other group tore down the original building and built a new structure, calling themselves The Calvary Baptist Church. I am certain that this development has been repeated in many other areas and among many denominations, not just Baptist.

Nonetheless, what the world sees is that church members care less about God's house than they do about their own houses. Then, when the church attempts outreach, it falls upon deaf ears. Revitalization becomes difficult because infighting happens to be a prominent feature and something for which the church is known. It is also a fact that people connect with the past through the worship center. Established churches oftentimes were designed, built, and maintained by former members, many of whom still have family in the church. To change the sanctuary equals discrediting the past.

Where Is the Main Entrance, Is It Visible, and Is There Adequate Signage?

I find how churches are built to be such an interesting study. Some churches, in order to make the entrance more accessible, build the church so that the back of the structure actually faces the main road. It is almost as if the church has turned its back on the community. Other churches, in order to have a visible front, build the church facing the road but with little or no access to this front entrance from the parking lot. How the building sets upon the property speaks volumes to newcomers. If they have a difficult time finding their way into the building, they may get back in their car and head home, or to another church.

Additionally, some churches have too many entrances. Because the buildings were not built through a master plan but seem to be piece-mealed together, no primary entrance exists. Thus, newcomers become confused as to where they are to enter the building.

Greeters and signage offer an easy fix for this problem. As overstated already, longtime members know which entrance to use and for what reasons. They know where the nursery is located and the best entrance for parents with children. Newcomers do not know these nuances and are often repelled or discouraged by such oversights. Therefore, if the entrances are difficult or multiple, adequate signage and an effective greeter team offer an immediate solution.

How Visible Is the Directional Church Signage?

When people drive up to the church, do they know where to park, where to enter, or where to find the nursery, the bathrooms, or the worship center? This problem can be easily and even inexpensively resolved, but it helps in understanding the perspective the present members have and the possible obstacles to church revitalization. It could well mean that the church really is not interested in new people attending. No one will publicly verbalize that idea, but the anecdotal evidence points otherwise.

When I pastored a small church with a sanctuary and a couple of rooms in the back, signage was not as essential. When I moved up to a church averaging over one hundred in attendance, even in this size church, signage was important. The building at this point was large enough that rooms were hidden, the nursery was difficult to find, and, outside of walking into the main sanctuary, no one really knew where anything else was located. The larger the buildings became, the more this problem was exasperated. I have even been in church facilities where I got lost the first time I went there. I have been at my church now well over a decade, and I still do not know where some things are located (a sad but true admission). Imagine how a first-time guest feels! Signage is important.

Parking

Church parking lots would offer some of the most comical looks at the congregation, if this issue was not so tragic at times. Obviously, churches are limited because of money and the size or shape of the property. Sometimes parking problems cannot be totally avoided due to circumstances outside the church's control. Yet many of the problems speak to the mind-set of the present church members.

Parking Assessment

Take a walk through the parking lot. If possible, watch the traffic flow and parking habits of the church members at large. Parking, along with where someone sits in the worship center, is a rite of passage. Years ago, I had one of my Younger Thirties tell me that he had to leave church quickly because he noticed his grandfather had pulled up to the church but then left. Upon arriving at his grandfather's home, he asked his grandparents if they were ill and needed to go to the doctor. The grandfather responded that neither of them was ill, but when they got to the church, someone had parked in his spot. He did not know what to do, so he came home. The grandson put them in his car and drove them to church—true story.

One of the evidences that church revitalization is needed can be determined by how and where people park. A church that holds to a mind-set of growth understands the need for newcomer parking and parking for parents of young children. This issue moves well beyond the fact that the church has signs designating this type of parking. It emanates from either a stakeholders mentality that refuses to acknowledge the need for insight and sacrifice when it comes to reaching new people, or from a Great Commission mind-set that not only understands but embraces the need to reach the unchurched. When a church loses its vision for growth, when challenges become problems, when people become self-centered or exist in self-protection modes, a clamoring occurs over parking.

I was at a restaurant recently and while waiting on the person with whom I was having lunch, I noticed an interesting event. The restaurant staff had placed a large sign on the door that said, "Closed" in large letters. Near the bottom in much smaller letters it read, "Thanksgiving Day." I watched as a car drove by the front door, obviously reading the sign, then drove away. A second car followed the same pattern. I mentioned to the greeter that they might want to redo their sign because people were seeing the part of the sign that read "Closed" but were not seeing the disclaimer.

Newcomers entering the church's parking lot might see the very same thing, except this time the sign reads, "Not Welcome." Churches might insist that they are open to new people, but the parking lot becomes the telltale sign. If no one provides them space to park, the word "Welcome" becomes superficial.

Staffing

One of the current models in church planting determines that proper staffing must be provided in advance, even before the church is planted. The sending church, organization, or board puts together a team that will be present from the day that the church launches, many of whom will be bi-vocational. This strategy offers several advantages, namely: support during difficult times, strategic thinking, shared ministry, and the ability to offer expanded ministry from the start of the church.

Churches in decline usually find themselves in a position of needing to lay off staff due to declining numbers and revenues. As a result, they have to cut ministries and stop doing some of the very things that would help them to stabilize and grow again. Usually it will be the age-graded or ministry-specific positions, such as the children's pastor or missions pastor, who will be the first to go. Thus, the church puts itself in a declining mode without really wanting to be in that position. The church plateaus, then starts a slow decline that cannot be reversed.

Staffing Assessment

Do a careful examination of the current staff positions, whether filled or open. The church may be so small that it cannot provide anything more than a part-time salary for the pastor. The remaining positions are filled by volunteers or are just left unfilled.

Questions to consider are:

1. Would the church be open to looking for God-called individuals to come in a bi-vocational capacity to help fill the voids?
2. What are the demographics of the church and what do these demographics necessitate regarding staffing? Sometimes churches are prone to automatically decide that the next position needed is a combination music/youth position, but that fact may not be necessarily so in all cases.
3. What demographic group will provide the greatest potential for outreach? The answer may lie in targeting a multicultural, multiethnic scenario. It could be that the greatest potential is in reaching twenty-somethings or baby boomers. Demographics will show what groups are moving in and moving out of the area

around the church. Staffing can be adapted to assist in reaching these groups.

Leadership Base

Sometimes churches fall into decline because the leadership base diminishes. Sunday school classes cease to exist because no teachers are available or no one is willing to serve. Committees are led by the same people or at least the same families because the church has stepped into a self-protective mode. Thirties view newcomers as threats or at least as people who will be at the church one day and then will leave tomorrow.

Leadership Base Assessment

Assessing this issue really begins with the pastor. For the long-term pastor, strong emotions often arise in thinking about revitalization. The new pastor may come in with visions of grandeur, only to find out that reality is much more difficult than the dream. A cycle of fear sets in, whereby the pastor begins to second-guess himself or his church. He starts to ask the "what ifs," doubting decisions made, even the decision to serve this particular church. This mode of thinking leads to an anxiousness that, in turn, results in a fear that it may be too late to leave. A desire to flee continues to permeate his thinking until some level of his fear becomes reality. He either burns out, runs out, or gets run out—none of which benefit the church.

The Pastor's Leadership Skills

As a pastor leading a church that needs revitalization or as a pastor considering this assignment, one must look at his own leadership capabilities and commitments. Some churches will be easier than others, but a steadfastness to stay and to thrive must be present in order for revitalization to take place.

John Maxwell has written a book that addresses what he determines to be the various levels or stages a person goes through in order to lead. These stages are listed from least effective to most effective. Maxwell writes,

How does leadership work? Unfortunately, people's usual answers . . . are not very helpful. Some people identify leadership with obtaining a leadership position. But I've known bad leaders who had good positions and good leaders who had no position at all. . . . Other people say of leadership, "I can't describe it but I know it when I see it." While that may be true, it doesn't help anyone learn how to lead. The conclusion I came to early on is that leadership is influence. If people can increase their influence with others, they can lead more effectively.[26]

These five levels of leadership are worth studying as a pastor. One may not necessarily agree with Maxwell's conclusion that "everything rises and falls on leadership,"[27] but his understanding of leadership is worth exploring and applying. Interpret these ideas in light of the servant-leader model presented in chapter 1.

Level 1: Lead by Position. One of the mistakes that many pastors make is when they believe that people will follow them, obey them, or listen to them because they hold the title "Pastor, Senior Pastor, or Lead Pastor." Titles are great, but people do not follow the pastor just because of the title. That fact holds true in most any organization. When the quarterback gets sacked and the offensive linemen do not help him up, he may be the quarterback, but he has yet to become the leader.

The pastor's ability to bring about change develops from something much greater than just position. In years past, the pastor's position carried more influence, but the church and the world have moved beyond this perspective of high esteem held by previous generations. Therefore, position becomes an even less impacting issue and sometimes a liability. He is still able to influence through his position, but that importance is usually among the very young. Teenagers on up could care less about position, degrees, and titles.

Level 2: Lead by Permission. In order for a pastor to receive permission to lead, three things need to happen:

1. Relationships have to be built.
2. Integrity has to be demonstrated.
3. Longevity has to be proven.

All of these characteristics prove to be important ingredients in a fruitful ministry, so there is nothing innately negative about this level of character development. As the pastor, though, one must lead from a far greater capability. The danger of staying at the permission level is that the pastor will become more concerned about pleasing people, especially pleasing the right people, rather than pleasing God. Therefore, the church never makes the changes it needs to make in order to revitalize because the stakeholders are not pleased by these modifications. The pastor's hands become tied because people will not be happy if he chooses to do what they do not like.

Level 3: Lead by Production. Once good relationships are built and those relationships move into credibility, they will often result in productivity. In the church, productivity can be seen in getting people to serve, give, and buy into the changes being made within the structure and functions of the church. Success has its benefits. When changes are initiated or when programs are eliminated or modified with resulting success, the pastor can initiate greater change. If those changes fail and a pattern of failure continues, then the opportunity to bring about revitalization diminishes.

This level of leadership offers a very positive side because it involves more people achieving the goals of the church than just the pastor. One of the difficulties of revitalization is that it is often begun alone. Therefore, build a ministry of integrity, develop relationships with people, and then involve these individuals in the ministries and the changes that must occur in order for revitalization to happen.

The negative of leading only through production, from a church standpoint, comes from the fact that the church and the pastor can lose their dependence upon God. Real production comes from Christ, not from us. John 15 clearly teaches that the disciple must stay connected to Christ, and when that fact occurs, the disciple will bear fruit, more fruit, and much fruit.[28] We can become too numbers-conscious at this point and very secular in our approach to church success.

Level 4: Lead by People Development. This level of leadership is critical to the church because it means that the pastor has learned to give the ministry away and to invest in others so that they, in turn, can do the work. It is precisely what Paul described in Ephesians 4:11–12, where he said, "And He personally gave some to be apostles, some prophets, some evangelists, some pastors and teachers, for the training of the saints in the work of the ministry, to build up the body of Christ."

Equipping the church and building up the body is revitalization. John MacArthur writes about this idea, "*Katartismos* (equipping) basically refers to that which is fit, is restored to its original condition, or is made complete. The word was often used as a medical term for the setting of bones. . . . *Oikodomē* (building up) literally refers to the building of a house, and was used figuratively of any sort of construction."[29] Certainly, we understand these concepts in spiritual development, but they definitely demonstrate for us clearly this level of necessary leadership in the pastor's life and ministry.

Church revitalization becomes the work of God, but He oftentimes uses people to accomplish His work. Thus, as the pastor equips people spiritually and for service, they become the instruments in God's hands to bring about change in the church. To accomplish this goal, however, requires a deep, spiritual commitment of the pastor and a willingness to take the time to equip and to invest. It demands far more than just preaching on Sundays or sending an occasional encouraging note. To equip the saints demands time and effort.

Level 5: The Pinnacle (Developing Leaders to Level 4). One of the reasons that I so enjoy teaching on the seminary level is because it allows me to influence the influencers. In talking with one of my deans, he was quite persuasive about how teaching at this level would make it possible for my ministry to extend well beyond my capabilities. If I did well in the classroom, the students, in turn, would impact the world.

That fact also rings true in the church. When the pastor becomes committed to equipping the saints, the next step is to develop them into believers who develop others. True discipleship happens when the one led to Christ is discipled in the faith enough so that he/she can disciple others. Out of that degree of discipleship come those whom God calls to serve Him in ministry and mission. In my opinion, one of the ways that a church knows that God's hand is upon them is when He calls out young people to serve Him in ministry. When God starts calling out the called, real revitalization is taking place.

As the leader of the church, the pastor must determine his own personal leadership level and skill. If leadership either assists or prevents revitalization, all who are interested in this art must determine where they stand in regard to leadership capabilities and make the commitment to grow spiritually so that they can influence the influencers.

The Church's Leadership Skills

The second part of this assessment is determining the leadership capabilities of the church. Oftentimes a pastor will arrive at a congregation in need of revitalization, and the truth is, the church has no leadership. Positions may be filled, but no spiritual leaders exist. A genuine lack of spiritual leadership becomes an incredible hindrance to the process of revitalization. It does not mean that revitalization is impossible. It just demonstrates one of the challenges faced by the pastor.

Step back to Levels 4 and 5 with regard to the leadership skills of the pastor, and the solution to this problem becomes viable. If the pastor does not have a passion for discipling people or does not have the drive to become the type of leader who trains people to become leaders, the lack of leadership and the problems associated with that lack of leadership will continue and will actually fester. It may be that a key reason that the church has declined comes from the fact that no one was training people to become spiritual leaders. Thus, a void now exists and the church remains stagnant because no spiritual leaders exist. I use the term "spiritual leaders" because the church is a spiritual body. Just because someone leads a Fortune 500 company does not mean that he/she can lead the church.

I found an article by Geoff Surratt to be quite helpful at this point. Here are some of the ideas he has discovered through his years in ministry and training.

- Not everyone is a leader. People can get training, but that training does not necessarily make them into a leader.
- Leadership classes do not develop leaders. At the end of the class, students become graduates, not leaders.
- Not all of the leadership sayings prove to be true: everything rises and falls on leadership; leaders are readers; leaders never eat alone.

Instead of doing seminars and training events for developing leaders, Surratt suggests training leaders the way that Jesus trained His disciples. If the pastor chooses this method, he obviously chooses to follow Levels 4 and 5 and to personally invest the time necessary to see people rise into spiritual leadership. Surratt explains about Jesus' leadership method, "He never held a class, he never put out a sign-up sheet, and there wasn't even a Starbucks in Galilee. But the eleven men he poured his life into changed the world."[30] According to Surratt, the method Jesus employed in building spiritual leaders includes these ideas:

1. **Jesus spent time observing potential leaders.** He spent time interacting with potential leaders in a variety of situations before tapping them for further development.
2. **Jesus handpicked His leaders.** No one self-selected into his group. Anyone could follow Jesus, but His inner circle was by invitation only.
3. **Jesus taught leadership along the way.** Rather than classrooms, books, and exercises, Jesus used birds, lilies, and farms to teach leadership. Leadership development was a natural outgrowth of being together.
4. **Jesus put His students into difficult leadership situations.** He constantly challenged them to lead beyond their comfort zones. ("How are you going to feed the crowd?" "Walk on water." "Go do miracles.")
5. **Jesus did not give His students a leadership template to follow; He gave them a mission to complete.** His final leadership instruction was to "Go make disciples."
6. **Jesus taught in public; He debriefed in private.** He often debriefed His public sermons in private with His students. They learned as much from the Q&A as they did from the original content.
7. **Jesus treated each leader as an individual.** He confronted Peter, He loved John, and He challenged Thomas.
8. **Jesus never kicked a leader out.** He challenged and corrected His students, but He never excommunicated them. Even Judas left on his own.

9. **Jesus spent three years developing twelve men.** He apparently could not come up with a mass program of microwave leadership development. Not only did His program take three years with twelve students, but it was 24/7/365. So if the Son of God poured every waking hour for three years into a class of twelve hand-picked leaders to achieved a 92% success rate, it is little wonder that we struggle developing leaders in six-week training classes.[31]

This step alone demonstrates why church revitalization is so difficult and why turning a church around takes time. It is also a reason for why many pastors never fulfill this task. It is difficult and it is time consuming. The church in need of revitalization needs strong pastoral leadership and effective spiritual leadership within the congregation. Hear the words of Ed Stetzer:

> Leadership is the most important factor in making a comeback. Leadership is rated as the factor having highest impact by comeback leaders. Leadership is about influence. Churches that are in a pattern of plateau or decline need strong leaders who will point the way to revitalization. . . . Comeback leaders identified several important components of leadership . . . the development of an attitude of growth, intentionality and proactivity, shared ministry, and the activation of a shared vision. . . . They are willing to identify and make necessary changes and set growth goals.[32]

The good news is that, if someone is willing to invest the time and invest in people, a good return is possible. Churches may be closing at an alarming rate, but some of those churches are salvageable. It just takes a pastor who is willing to take the risk to lead the church to revitalize. Effective church revitalization probably will take, at the minimum, seven to ten years. Here is what the process may look like:

- Years 1 and 2: prep time for establishing biblical parameters and priorities, developing core values, and formulating the vision for the church
- Years 2 and 3: implementing structural changes, ongoing leadership development, and communicating the vision of the church

- Years 4 and 5: completing changes in structure, developing and aligning ministries that assist the church in achieving its vision, dealing with festered problems both that were already in the church and have arisen due to the implemented changes and vision (years 4–7 are the crisis years in the church)
- Years 6 and 7: continuing to resolve problems, recognizing that the preacher has now become the pastor, ongoing leadership development, furthering the alignment of ministries
- Years 7 to 10: reestablishing the vision of the church, reviewing biblical parameters and priorities, reviewing structure and ministry needs

Be willing to invest the time necessary and use that time wisely (Eph. 4:15–16).

Assimilation

Note these statistics from various researchers that show the importance of assimilation. People leave the church:

- Within the first two years of joining
- Between the ages of fifteen and twenty-three
- When they go through the empty-nest syndrome
- After a divorce

Assimilation serves one of the more difficult tasks for any church. Some churches have enough new people visit and join so that retention is not a huge issue. If they have more people coming in than going out, the numbers look good and basic growth occurs. For the church needing revitalization, that luxury is usually not an option, especially if the church is located in a more stable or even declining area. Fewer people visit and join the church, therefore, the need for assimilation becomes a much greater issue. The average church in America sees only 12 percent of first-time guests return the following Sunday and, in turn, become members. A few congregations have 20 to 25 percent retention but few churches surpass the 30 percent mark.[33] The fact is, very few churches are actually achieving what would be considered healthy growth. Healthy growth can be defined as:

- The church experiences consistent growth over a five-year period, not just one or two years.
- The church baptismal rate is 35:1, meaning that the church baptizes 1 person for every thirty-five members.
- Growth occurs whereby conversions provide at least 25% of the annual growth.[34]

Assimilation can be understood in several ways. Ron Jenson and Jim Stevens refer to assimilation as a type of absorption, explaining that it is "the process by which people are taken into the life of the church and by which a strong sense of identity and belonging develops."[35] Measuring this process occurs during the "length of time between the first visit and the application for membership and complete commitment to the church."[36] Elmer Towns uses the term "bonding" to better define assimilation.[37]

Various lists are available for evaluating assimilation effectiveness, but perhaps Joel Heck offers one of the most comprehensive. A Christian genuinely assimilated into the church will possess most of the following qualities:

1. Identifies with the goals of the church.
2. Is regular in worship attendance and in attendance at special services (Heb. 10:25).
3. Attends Communion and Sunday school regularly and has Bible reading and family devotions in the home (Acts 2:42).
4. Attends some special functions of the congregation, such as council meetings, church picnics, special workshops, and midweek services.
5. Is growing spiritually (2 Pet. 3:18).
6. Has affiliated with the congregation.
7. Has six or more friends in the church.
8. Has a task or role that is appropriate for his or her spiritual gift(s) (Rom. 12; 1 Cor. 12; Eph. 4; 1 Pet. 4:10–11).
9. Is involved in a fellowship group (Acts 2:42).
10. Gives regularly and generously (1 Cor. 16:2).
11. Tells others about the Lord and His church (Matt. 28:18–20; Acts 1:8).[38]

Assimilation

One can easily determine how well the church assimilates its members by asking a few simple questions and examining the evidence. Additionally, the majority of these ideas can be easily implemented immediately into the life of the church.

How Effectively Does the Church Attract Guests and Is There a Culture to Do So?

The word *hospitality*, as it is used in Scripture, means "a love of strangers."[39] If most pastors asked their congregations if they were friendly, the churches would respond with a resounding "Yes!" What they mean, however, is that they are friendly to one another. When they arrive at the church meeting place, they have the friends that they know and engage them in conversation. Most Christians do not intend on being cliquish, but the fact is that this dilemma affects all age groups. We gravitate to people we know and like.

One of the reasons that people do not return to the church is because of a lack of immediate connection. Friendliness that leads to assimilation is a culture, and it is a constant battle in the church. We all tend to return to the familiar if not reminded to look beyond ourselves. Begin teaching the church these ideas:

- Do not mistreat newcomers in the church. Asking them to stand, recognizing them as visitors, or asking them to introduce themselves in the service (yes, I have seen this practice done) mistreats those who are first-time guests.
- Treat newcomers as if they were a part of your own family. If a member of your family visited the church one Sunday, how would you treat them? Therefore, greet them with a genuine enthusiasm, invite them to join you and others for lunch afterward, or just make yourself available to answer questions or give directions.
- Remember what it feels like to be new. The problem we face in making newcomers feel welcome is that we have forgotten what it was like to be new. Encourage church members to visit a new church while on vacation and take some mental notes on what

takes place and how they feel. It is a fearful thing to visit a church for the first time, even if a newcomer attends with a friend or family member. This fear is compounded especially for those who do not know Christ.

- Understand that the church cannot grow without new people. Biological growth will barely sustain a church, much less make it grow. Add to this fact that young people are not staying in their respective churches because of being far more mobile than their parents, and the problem multiplies.

In leading the church to develop a culture of welcoming guests, the pastor can take some strategic steps that will help members to invite their friends and acquaintances and will welcome people when they come. Oftentimes, churches in need of revitalization think that it will be impossible to do anything because of limited finances, but several opportunities afford themselves to any church of any size and capabilities.

Preach about and Pray for New People to Come to Church. I have mentioned preaching often in this book because of its power to disciple people and to create a Great Commission mind-set. Unfortunately, we have been guilty of preaching irrelevant sermons. Preach for change and conviction about reaching those who do not know Christ. Make this issue a focus of intentional prayer times. It may require starting out small, but when people are led to pray about or hear prayers about having a passion for those who are not believers, some will catch the fire.

Provide Opportunities for Church Members to Invite Their Friends. In years past, I was very involved in witness training and door-to-door visitation. In most communities, these methods have become less effective. A few exceptions still exist, but most people are not receptive to having someone come to their door uninvited. It does not mean that evangelism is ineffective; it simply means that new methods must be employed. Here are a few suggestions:

- **Implement a strategy of servant evangelism.** One of the problems facing the church is an image problem. The church for too long has been known for asking the community, "What can you do for us?" rather than letting people know that "the church exists for the community." Steve Sjogren wrote a great little book in 2000 entitled *101 Ways to Reach Your Community*.[40] It lists 101 ways to do servant evangelism. Do a one-day Servant Evangelism Blitz, sending the church out into the community to meet needs (develop projects ahead of time). Involve the church's Sunday school classes in building relationships in the community so that they can conduct ongoing ministry. Work with local schools with no strings attached. Do not demand that church material be distributed or even shirts worn with the church's name. Just go and serve. Those other opportunities will arise as trust is built.

- **Teach people how to build witnessing relationships.** While this idea might seem rather unnecessary since everyone has friendships, the fact is that most people have not developed witnessing relationships. They do not witness, not because they hate Christ or because they are closet universalists, but because they are afraid. Evangelism involves spiritual warfare, and most Christians are not ready for it or do not understand it. Teach believers how to build relationships with people they do not know. Include in the teaching how to move the conversation from the secular to the spiritual. Tim Beougher's book, *Overcoming Walls to Witnessing*,[41] is a great tool for accomplishing this task. One of the things that has changed dramatically over the last several decades is the ease and acceptance in inviting people to attend some kind of worship experience. People have a lot more barriers today than before, therefore, having a personal relationship with someone that can lead to a witnessing relationship helps tremendously.

- **Provide opportunities for people to invite others to church.** Teach Sunday school classes to utilize fellowships as an introduction for newcomers to church life. Encourage them to have some of their fellowships off-campus, with the understanding that unchurched friends will be invited to attend. Preach sermon series that will disciple believers but also be interesting to those who do not know Christ. Advertise these series weeks in advance. Provide some simple cards that will allow members to invite people to a worship service or to a specific sermon series. The back of the card should include a map, directions, and contact information. Also, utilize a card that people can keep in their

Bibles or in their wallets where they can write down the names of others whom they want to invite to a service and engage in conversation about Christ. Nelson Searcy offers some very good suggestions about attractional evangelism activities in his book *Ignite*.[42] While I do not subscribe to the idea that the only evangelism that should be done is inviting people to a worship service or that this method replaces personal evangelism, it is an effective way to introduce newcomers to the gospel. It also becomes a first step for non-witnessing Christians to be open to the next phase of evangelism.

Develop a User-Friendly Website. In today's technological world, people will first check out a church on the web before visiting. People rarely consult the Yellow Pages first. Even senior adults are becoming computer savvy, or at least computer literate. In years past, developing and maintaining a website was incredibly expensive and was not practical for smaller churches or ones on a tight budget.

Today, those costs have significantly decreased. Therefore, it behooves the revitalization pastor to examine the church's website and make improvements. If the website needs an overhaul, take the time to bring it about. A good website does not need to be complicated. Look at the Google home page. It is probably the most simple of any website out there. Yet, it is functional and obviously popular for what it does.

Here are some suggestions for simplicity's sake:

- Have the worship times and locations clearly visible
- Use a simple domain name for your church
- Have a map available for directions
- Include information about yourself and your staff but do not make it look like a résumé
- Upload sermons and list the current sermon series
- Include contact information, including e-mail addresses and the physical address of the church
- Make navigating the website simple. Use easy links to other pages. If someone has to navigate through several pages to get to needed information, that person will not stay on the website for very long.

Forbes Magazine observes that the human brain makes a thousand computations the moment strangers meet. They explain, "And these computations are made at lightning speed. Researchers from NYU found that we make eleven major decisions about one another in the first seven seconds of meeting."[43] Apply that idea to a website. It will not take long for someone to leave a church's website if the sought information is difficult to find, out of date, or not available at all. In the end, people may have a negative attitude toward the church if the website is hard to navigate or if it is nonexistent.

What Kind of Follow-Up Does the Church Do with First-Time Guests?

Every church should have the goal to contact guests within forty-eight hours of their visit. This process increases the possibility of a return visit greatly. Sometimes the pastor might encounter hesitancy to this type of ministry because some will retort that people need to make that decision on their own. While it is true that the church should not manipulate or pressure people into a decision of any kind, do not forget the passion that Christ tells believers to have with regard to those who do not know Him in Luke 14:23. Think of Paul for a moment. He wrote, "For I could almost wish to be cursed and cut off from the Messiah for the benefit of my brothers, my own flesh and blood" (Rom. 9:3). Reformer John Calvin explained the meaning of these words in Paul's mind:

> He could not have expressed a greater ardour of love than by what he testifies here; for that is surely perfect love which refuses not to die for the salvation of a friend. But there is another word added, *anathema,* which proves that he speaks not only of temporal but of eternal death; and he explains its meaning when he says, *from Christ,* for it signifies a separation. And what is to be separated from Christ, but to be excluded from the hope of salvation? It was then a proof of the most ardent love, that Paul hesitated not to wish for himself that condemnation which he saw impending over the Jews, in order that he might deliver them. It is no objection that he knew that his salvation was based on the election of God, which could by no means fail; for as those ardent feelings hurry us on impetuously, so they see and regard

nothing but the object in view. So Paul did not connect God's election with his wish, but the remembrance of that being passed by, he was wholly intent on the salvation of the Jews.[44]

I am not certain that anyone can fully understand the passion that Paul possessed. How could he desire that he would give up his own salvation so that others could be saved? Yet, that is exactly what he says. That same love should compel every Christian, and it behooves the church to do whatever it takes to share the gospel and to reach the nonbeliever.

Building churches is like building houses. We must establish our churches on the foundation of Christ and Who He is. The walls that connect the church together come out of our theology. We must lead our churches to have a solid, biblical understanding of how we do church. The roof that connects the entire church, however, is evangelism. *Evangelism is the barometer of our theology.* In other words, if a person's theology does not lead to having a passion for doing evangelism, that individual needs to get a new theology. The same idea holds true for the church. If the church does not have a strong theology that leads to evangelism, the pastor then knows some of the preparatory work that must be done before the church will begin to reach those outside of Christ. This one thought may be the entire reason that the church has declined and is in need of revitalization. Without a strong theology of evangelism, the church finds itself on the precipice of a slippery slope that affects every work and every ministry of the church. Get the evangelistic fervor right and the church begins to head in the correct direction.

In order for the church to reach newcomers, an aggressive strategy should be adopted and followed. Without new people coming into the church, the church will eventually die. On average, churches will lose people:

- 2% by death (older congregations obviously will have a much higher percentage
- 4% by transfer to other churches
- 6% by inactivity or by dropping out[45]

Thus, if a church is not replacing 10 to 12 percent of its membership each year, it then begins to plateau and eventually to fall into decline, especially as these percentages increase due to age or demographic changes. Here are some suggestions for effective follow-up of newcomers.

Recognize that Follow-Up Begins the Moment a Person Steps onto the Church Campus.

Many churches make the mistake of thinking that follow-up begins once a person has left the building. The mind-set, though, that the church must adopt is that follow-up begins once a person drives into the parking lot. It has already been discussed in detail about signage, visible parking spaces, and property condition. These things are the first impressions that a person has even before meeting anyone in the church. It is for these reasons also that parking teams, greeter teams, and ushers provide such an important ministry to newcomers. They are of great significance. As already noted, they actually are the most important service committees that the church has.

Establish Intentional Touches That Minister to Newcomers and Communicate Effectively the Church's Mission.

Ten Suggested Touches of the Church

1. First Contact: Arriving on Sunday for worship or Sunday school
   - The guest is greeted with a warm and personal greeting in the parking lot and at whatever door through which they may enter.
2. Second Contact: During worship or Sunday school
   - Members in worship or Sunday school are aware of those around them so the guest will sense a warmth and sincerity in their hospitality.
3. Third Contact: Contact with the pastor at the Welcome Center
   - Guests receive a gift bag from the pastor at the welcome center. It is suggested that guests turn in their registration tabs if one is completed.
   - Suggested gift bag items:
     - A CD of the church's vision as preached by the pastor
     - A letter welcoming guests to the church

   ¤ Simple items with the church's name and information such as:
- * Pens (Do not give the huge, thick ones. An inexpensive pen works well and people will carry them)
- * Hand sanitizer with church logo
- * Refrigerator magnets with church logo
- * Car sunglass holder with church logo
- * A Bible (LifeWay Christian Stores and other bookstores sell inexpensive New Testaments)
- * A brochure about the church's ministries

4. Fourth Contact: Registration tabs[46] or Sunday school forms are turned into the office
   - On that Sunday afternoon or evening, a deacon will take a loaf of bread to the family simply to say, *"Thank you for attending church today."*

5. Fifth Contact: During the week after their visit to worship
   - A personal, handwritten note from the Senior Pastor is sent to express, *"Thanks for worshiping with us today."*
   - If the person indicated that he/she would like more information on the church, a detailed brochure is mailed to that person.

6. Sixth Contact: During second week after their initial visit
   - The Discipleship Pastor or Sunday School Director will follow up with a phone call or card inviting them to Sunday school or encouraging them to enroll in the group that meets their particular age group or need.
   - If the person indicated that he/she would like a personal visit, an appointment is scheduled for a visit to be made.

7. Seventh Contact: The second or third week after their initial visit
   - Phone call from the Sunday school teacher or class care leader inviting them to come to their class (or thanking them for attending if they have already attended).

8. Eighth Contact: The fourth week after initial visit
   - Follow-up phone call or card from the Sunday school teacher or class care leader checking to see how the church can help them.

9. Ninth Contact: The fourth week after initial visit
  - Newsletter sent to guest so information about the church, current activities, and ministries will be communicated effectively.
10. Tenth Contact: Ten to twelve weeks after initial visit
  - Phone call from Staff Member or Teacher/Leader to make sure the individual or family is still connecting well with the church.

How Many Connection Points Are Available for New People?

While a worship service offers an initial contact with the church, if it is the only connection point that a newcomer has, the tie probably will not last long. People need to connect with others in order to develop a desire to be a part of the church. If relationships are what bring people to church, then relationships must be established in order for that bond to continue.

A popular word in today's church culture is *community*. People need community. They need a place where they can be loved, accepted, challenged, and encouraged. Community, regardless of what it has been termed in the past, has been a primary need for human beings ever since God created Adam and Eve. The classic verse of Scripture that defines this perspective is Acts 4:32, "Now the large group of those who believed were of one heart and mind, and no one said that any of his possessions was his own, but instead they held everything in common." Even the Old Testament speaks of this need, "Two are better than one because they have a good reward for their efforts. For if either falls, his companion can lift him up; but pity the one who falls without another to lift him up" (Eccl. 4:9–10). In order for the church to reach new people, a process that in turn will lead to revitalization, community must be established. The following are some suggestions:

New Member/Church Information Class. Several years ago I read Chuck Lawless's book entitled *Membership Matters*. Among the many ideas that I gleaned from his book, one of those was the importance of conducting a regular New Member Class. I was especially convicted about my personal role in teaching and leading the class. I had always believed that a New Member Class was important, and I had established one in the current church that I was serving. The problem came through my involvement. I asked my Discipleship Pastor to teach the class, and I would show up during the time that the class was meeting to introduce myself and answer any quick questions. The whole process took maybe fifteen minutes.

Then I read Lawless's book. In it, he writes,

> On the basis of our research, we strongly encourage the senior pastors to teach membership classes. Pastors embody the church's vision, and they are most often the driving force behind it. They bring to the class a passion and commitment few others in the church have. . . . Pastors who do not lead the classes may miss a prime opportunity to influence church members for years to come. Even a few hours of personal interaction can make a difference.[47]

What I immediately realized about a New Member Class was that it provided a great way to introduce people from all kinds of backgrounds to the vision of the church. Therefore, instead of just calling it the New Member Class, call it the Discover Class. That way, people who have not joined yet, those who are new members, and people who have been members for a number of years can be invited to attend. The information that is taught is simple but helpful. The material includes:

- An introduction of all staff members and a brief understanding of their responsibilities
- An explanation of how the church functions and the roles of the primary leaders within the church
- A definition and explanation of church membership, with a listing of a specific church covenant
- An overview of the mission statement of the church
- An explanation of Sunday school/Discipleship and how those ideas function
- An explanation of the vision of the church and how that vision can assist in the discipleship process
- A spiritual gifts inventory
- An explanation of ways that people can serve within the church
- An overview of the church budget
- A explanation of the specifics of church theology and practice

Use a spiritual gift inventory[48] and connect those gifts with the areas of service that are available in the church. One of the changes we have made is to distinguish between administrative teams that must be elected by the church and service teams that allow people to volunteer for and serve on immediately. Doing the inventory allows people to find where they ought to be serving and in what areas they would find the most fulfillment. Too often, people serve out of guilt or need but are not gifted for that particular ministry. Sometimes because of a lack of leadership or even bodies, people have to take jobs in the church for which they are not necessarily suited. The hopeful goal of the Discover Class is that more people will be quickly empowered to serve.

What we have also found is that by offering the spiritual gift inventory, it has encouraged longtime members to attend. We can offer the class more often because attendance is better with the expanded number of prospects for the class. This fact becomes especially true after I preach a sermon on service or the need to know our spiritual gifting. The Word stirs people's hearts to serve, and the Discover Class helps to provide a way for them to get connected. The class itself takes about three hours to teach, with breaks, dinner, and questions.

Sunday School Classes. An established church provides a unique advantage over the new church start in many ways. Sometimes pastors view church revitalization as an extremely negative ministry. Yet, in spite of the challenges, several benefits are present.

First, an established church will usually have some type of organization in place. It probably needs tweaking and may need a complete overhaul in some cases, but the positive side is that people are accustomed to an organizational structure.

Second, an established church has a ready-made building that probably has sufficient space for doing discipleship and worship. Granted, the space may need some updating, but the cost of making simple improvements far outweighs the cost of new construction.

Third, an established church will oftentimes have a Sunday morning discipleship ministry in place. Many of these churches call this discipleship organization Sunday school. Some within this era of post-modernity (and perhaps post-Christian culture) often criticize and even ridicule the idea of Sunday school. Granted, some Sunday schools exist that do not accomplish the task for which they were created. They do not disciple, build fellowship, or attract new people. That fact, however, should not detract from recognizing the huge benefit that a Sunday school can provide in offering connection points for people. My love for the Sunday school comes partly out of the depth and expanse of its discipleship possibilities. It also stems from the percentage of worship attenders who are connected to discipleship. As a staff, we set a goal of having at least 80 percent of our worship attendance involved in a discipleship group. That goal offers one way that we can determine the health of our church and how easy it will be to cast vision and make changes. If people are being discipled, they are developing skills in hermeneutics, application, evangelism, and a host of other learning opportunities. Many develop a missional perspective, as we encourage every class to start a class. This idea stirs people toward outreach, connection, and even evangelism. When new people join the church, an immediate connection results as Sunday school teachers and members invite them to be a part of their classes. It is not a perfect system and some classes do not perform their functions at full capacity, but the benefits far outweigh anything negative that someone might think about Sunday school.

I understand why many new church starts do not offer Sunday school. They do not have the leadership, teachers, or facilities to be able to accomplish this task. The established church has an advantage. The facilities are already in place. Several people in the church are already skilled or have experience in teaching a small group. The church is already organized for such a ministry. The people just need a leader who can show them how the Sunday school can help the church to revitalize. It will take some time, some strong preaching and teaching, but the possibilities are present. Thus, the Sunday school becomes a positive means by which new people can find a connection point.

Service Opportunities. One of the current discussions that I have with others relating to church polity and ecclesiology surrounds the idea of [Believe °Belong °Become] or [Belong°Believe°Become]. Part of the discussion involves nomenclature (i.e., the meaning of the particular words). In my definition, I see *belonging* as explaining the process by which a person becomes a part of the body of Christ, not just a fellowship group of the church. Therefore, an individual must first *believe*, meaning that he/she has repented of personal sin and has trusted in Christ as Savior. Then that person is able to *belong* to the body of Christ, an experience that is partly expressed through the public confession of a person's faith through baptism. Where most of us agree, though, is that to *belong* also means that a person gets connected to the local church. How that process happens is a genuine challenge for most churches.

One area that provides great assistance in assimilating new people into the church is through service. The questions that every pastor has to settle are:

1. At what level can new people serve? What type of structure does the church have in service opportunities and are there different levels of importance or leadership within those service groups? Some groups, committees, or teams might wield less power or have fewer spiritual demands and thus provide opportunities for a new person to serve immediately.

2. At what stage in their church attendance/membership are people allowed to serve? Some churches require that, for any service committee or team, a person has to be a member. Others will add that a person has to have been a member for at least a year or even two before serving the church. Every church and every pastor has to answer those questions, taking into consideration the church's procedures and doctrine. A balance, nevertheless, can be struck.

Typical Procedures for Serving. When it comes to serving, churches struggle more with polity than theology. Many churches operate from a somewhat antiquated system made up of committees that serve and those that choose who will serve. Most autonomous denominations, state and private universities, and even government agencies and congressional bodies also operate in this same manner.

The system works in this way. A Nominating Committee is chosen by the Church Moderator or some leadership group. The Nominating Committee then chooses who will serve on the Committee on Committees. A twist that adds greater drama to this scenario occurs when self-perpetuation is included in the equation. This process takes place when the Nominating Committee elects the Committee on

Committees that, in turn, elects the Nominating Committee. The problems created by this system can be multiple, but two critical issues come to mind:

1. It opens the door for power struggles to take place. If the Thirties rule the CoC and the NomC, a possible catastrophe brews if they are not on board with change and revitalization. The interests become centered more on maintaining power than on helping the church to survive and thrive. In fact, resistance to growth increases because new people represent a threat to their position and power.

2. It limits who can and will serve because people are limited in the number of individuals with whom they are familiar and can nominate for a position. The obvious hope is that, with a large number of people serving, they will be able to pick from a large segment of the church. This idea looks good on paper, but it rarely works in reality.

A Potential Alternative

If the church follows this particular pattern of polity, changing it will be difficult. Later in the book, a process is presented that offers a possible matrix for bringing about change in the church. I wish I could say that the change will be painless and without any repercussions, but I am not naïve enough to believe that change can happen without some consequences. When done with wisdom and patience, it can be as painless as possible.

One important change to consider involves the organizational structure of the church in how it elects people to serve. Here is a possible process that will allow for church input in the election of leaders but also provide ways for new people to connect to the church and to progress toward assimilation.

Divide the Church Committees into Three Groups

Many Thirties fear allowing the inexperienced or the immature to serve in areas that require leadership, wisdom, and spiritual maturity. Granted that they themselves may not fit those descriptions, but in most cases, their concern is legitimate and reasonable. Therefore, one of the ways to alleviate these fears is by making a clear distinction between administrative committees, service committees/ministries, and teaching ministries.

Administrative committees are those teams that lead the church by making particular decisions for the church. One way to make this change is by leading the church to establish certain spiritual criteria for serving on an Administrative Committee. This decision will encourage the Thirties to understand the importance of and the protective nature of this change. Administrative committees include groups such as Personnel, Finance, Leadership or the Church Council, and Trustees (if the church is incorporated). Particular churches may have other committees that also fall in this category.

Have a Specific Process for Electing the Administrative Committees

In order to break up power groups but also allow for a shared ministry that invites the input of laypeople, develop a system that encourages pastors and church members to work together. Both pastors and church leaders must move beyond the "us versus them" mentality that exists in so many churches. Sometimes this attitude has legitimate roots due to the failure of both those in ministry and in lay leadership. Church people must, however, determine that neither the pastor nor the church member is the enemy. Satan is the enemy. Paul writes, "For our battle is not against flesh and blood, but against the rulers, against the authorities, against the world powers of this darkness, against the spiritual forces of evil in the heavens" (Eph. 6:12).

Preaching, modeling, and explaining this fact serve as a prerequisite to bringing about this type of change. Let the people know that the pastor is on their side. Occasionally pastors go into churches with a combative spirit, forgetting that the church is not the enemy. Settle the issue of who runs the church first (Jesus), and then bring about change.

A suggested process for electing leaders is as follows:

- Lead the pastor(s) and the deacon officers to serve as a Nominating Committee that, in turn, nominate those who will serve on the Church Council or Leadership Team.

- The Leadership Team with the pastor(s) then nominates those who serve on the remaining Administrative Committees. The obvious downfall of this idea is that those doing the nominating are still limited in knowing a large cross-section of people. The positive side is that those available to serve, especially if the church requires specific criteria for administrative service, will be limited more to those who are actively involved in the church and have proven themselves to many people. If the church is elder-led, the staff elders and the lay elders can serve in place of the pastors and the deacon officers.
- If the church is accustomed to voting on its leaders, bring these names before the church for vote. Explain the process and the criteria for service, clarifying the biblical model for leadership and how these individuals are believed to meet these requirements.

Align All Committees and Ministries to Help the Church Accomplish Its Goals

An important part of this plan is that all committees/ministries, including administrative, service, and teaching, must help the church to reach its goals and fulfill its mission. Chapter 14, explaining the Change Matrix, encourages the church to develop biblical priorities, a mission statement, and a purpose statement. These priorities and statements must set the tone for why service teams exist. Often people do not serve because most committees only meet. They never serve. In today's culture, new members, especially Millennials, do not want to attend meetings; they want to be involved in something significant. The development of these priorities and statements assists in keeping the church on target and in communicating to people the direction of the church.

Some churches define the mission and purpose statements synonymously. Others, myself included, see the mission statement as a compound sentence that defines the specific direction or vision of a church. The mission statement begins by saying, "Calvary Church[49] exists to . . . or the mission of Calvary Church is to. . . ." It serves as the *how* of the church. The purpose statement is a far more simple sentence that offers a type of slogan that defines the *why* of the church. For example, one mission statement reads: *Our mission is to worship God, to globally lead people*

to faith in Christ, and to grow together to be like Him. The purpose statement simply says: *We are a home for your heart with a heart for the world.*[50]
The book *Simple Church*, coauthored by Thom Rainer and Eric Geiger,
provides a very important resource at this point. The book's basic premise is that a church needs to get simple in its ministries and programs in
order to grow. Many churches have so many activities that nothing connects those things together, and the church actually becomes ineffective.
Therefore, a church has to learn to get smaller in order to get larger by
culling those interests that are nonessential or that do not help the church
accomplish its mission. The process Rainer and Geiger suggest involves
the following ideas:

- Clarity: Starting with a Ministry Blueprint
- Movement: Removing Congestion
- Alignment: Maximizing the Energy of Everyone
- Focus: Saying No to Almost Everything[51]

All of these ideas work together in harmony by helping the church
stay focused on its primary mission: reaching people. At times, it may
seem that the concept intends to run off a number of people and ministries. As with any book, process, or program, church leaders need to
show caution in how they introduce and incorporate these ideas into the
church. In many situations, if leaders will meet with those who direct
or oversee particular ministries, they will find that giving the ministry
purpose and connection with the entire church will align those ministries
and leaders with the church's direction. No alignment has taken place
because no guidance has been given and no opportunity has ever been
afforded to do so.

Colin Marshall and Tony Payne make a similar plea for the church
to move to a ministry mind-shift that helps the church fulfill the Great
Commission of making disciples. They proffer that certain shifts must
happen in the church, as it moves from:

- Running programs to building people
- Running events to training people
- Using people to growing people
- Filling gaps to training new workers

- Solving problems to helping people make progress
- Clinging to ordained ministry to developing team leadership
- Focusing on church polity to forging ministry partnerships
- Relying on training institutions to establishing local training
- Focusing on immediate pressures to aiming for long-term expansion
- Engaging in management to engaging in ministry
- Seeking church growth to desiring gospel growth[52]

While not everyone will agree with all that Marshall and Payne suggest in this list (their idea of doing leadership training conflicts somewhat with Geoff Surratt's proposal), their ideas demonstrate the benefit of alignment and purpose. The church in need of revitalization must come together in one movement that brings unity to the congregation in purpose, focus, direction, and goal. The Scripture asks, "Can two walk together without agreeing to meet?" (Amos 3:3). The immediate context of that verse applies to God's special relationship with Israel and the responsibilities required within that relationship. The simplicity of the proverb relates also to life in general and to the church. Two people do not travel together unless they have met and agreed on the travel plans, including the destination.[53] If believers are not in unity and one in purpose as God's people, they will never achieve the ultimate intention that God has for them. They might see individual victories, but for the church in need of revitalization, oneness in direction and purpose is an absolute necessity. In other words, the church has to meet together in order to determine travel plans, routes, and directions so that the members, ministries, and service teams can walk together and reach the final destination. A traveler alone risks great danger from robbers and thieves. The church that does not walk together cannot withstand the attacks of the Enemy and dies (John 10:10).

Service committees need to be evaluated as to their effectiveness, challenged to align with and to assist the church in reaching its goals, culled when unnecessary or redundant, and developed so that new people can get connected and bring life to the fledgling congregation.

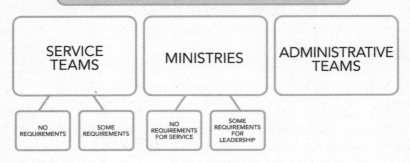

Develop a Strategy to Help People Connect

Once the committees/ministries are structured and aligned, develop a strategy for promoting these teams and ministries, incorporating ways for people to connect in serving. Divide the service committees into two groups. Just as the Administrative Committees require people who have a longer track record and spirituality in the church, some of the service committees may have some, if not all, of those same requirements. A counting committee (those who take care of counting the Sunday offerings) might necessitate that its members have a solid record of giving, along with a proven accountability. The same idea applies to ministries. While anyone can be involved in these ministries, leadership for some may demand a longer tenure of membership. The church needs to determine the specific criteria for these teams.

Other committees, though, will provide an immediate means by which new people can immediately connect. For example:

- The Parking Team
- Ushers
- Offering Team
- Welcome Center Helpers
- Hospitality Team
- Greeters
- Bereavement Team

- Missions Team
- Set-up Crew
- Shut-in Ministry
- Recreation Team
- Baptismal/Lord's Supper Team
- Worship Service Counselors
- Property Maintenance Team

The list can go on but make sure that each team fits the church's mission statement.

Follow a Basic Plan. Once a mission statement is in place, encourage service teams and ministries to help fulfill that mission purpose. For example, the mission statement, *to worship God, to globally lead people to faith in Christ, and to grow together to be like Him,* has three important sections: *worship, lead,* and *grow.* Train teams and ministries to fulfill at least one part of the mission statement, if not two. Then, in meeting with those teams and ministries, accountability and evaluation becomes much easier. The teams align better to the church's focus because specific reasons are given for their existence. Leaders find that they now have a purpose in what they do and sense that they are a greater part of the church. Through this process, the pastor builds consensus for change, along with providing necessary ingredients for moving the church toward revitalization. People resist change because they feel abandoned or ignored. They want to believe and even feel that their work is not just important but is recognized by the church and the church staff. When these ministries or teams are marginalized, they become isolated and possibly hostile. Therefore, the pastor must lead the church to evaluate the effectiveness of its work, teams, and ministries; eliminate those that are not helping the church to fulfill its mission; and align those teams with a greater sense of need and responsibility to help the church achieve its mission purpose.

Conduct a Ministry Fair. Once a year, lead the church to have a Ministry Fair, in which all the ministries and service teams that do not require election by the church or any leadership prerequisites are highlighted. Preach on service, ministry, and mission on Sunday morning, explaining the process for the Ministry Fair. Then release the church to serve. People can be given additional opportunities to join a ministry as New Member classes are offered throughout the year.

The first time that this fair is conducted, people may have a difficult time trying to figure out how to serve. They have been used to a system where they have been asked to serve and cannot understand how they can just volunteer. It requires a huge mind-set change, especially in the established church, so do not get discouraged if people do not immediately rush to join a team or ministry. The first year may still require personal enlistment and phone calls.

As time passes and as the church embraces this concept, people will begin to anticipate the Ministry Fair and the opportunities to join another service team or to find out more information on a particular ministry in the church. This acceptance and understanding will take some time, especially since the Ministry Fair is conducted only once a year. Be patient, make necessary adjustments, and keep focused.

It is important to make the Ministry Fair fun and exciting. Here are some suggested ideas for it success:

- Do it in the early evening a few weeks before the school year begins. Summer is best because the weather is nice and some activities can be done outside.
- Make it family friendly. Encourage people to dress casually and bring their children. Make access into the building easier for strollers and crowds.
- Have activities for the kids. Designate certain areas for children to play games or have opportunities that involve them personally.
- Provide food if possible. It does not need to be anything elaborate—hot dogs, chips, and sodas. People will be more likely to come if they can eat.
- Have each ministry and committee/team represented at a table/booth, specifically decorated for that work. Include information about what that team does, how often it serves, and what gifts or talents might fit that particular group. Have a sign-up list on the table so that people can immediately join the group. Make sure that those individuals are contacted within a reasonable amount of time.
- Conduct the Ministry Fair with a specific start time and end time. Make the sign-up tables, information, and sign-up lists available for a few weeks after the Ministry Fair. This process

allows the church to continue to publicize its ministries but also allows for those who were not able to attend to get connected.

The ultimate goal is to have a Ministry Fair annually but also to have a process in place whereby new people can immediately connect. For example, if a new person has to wait a year before joining a service team, it might become a great hindrance to serving. The New Member Class or Discover Class can help during the interim between fairs. At that meeting, encourage people to sign up or to consider signing up within the next few weeks. Emphasize how the church expects and needs all members to serve; then provide the means.

Determine Which Teams/Ministries Do Not Require Membership. Most of the church teams and ministries will require membership in the church in order to serve. There may be some, however, that will allow those who are exploring membership to go ahead and serve without having yet joined the church.

If the church expects membership (some churches do not have any kind of membership requirements, rolls, or expectations), be careful about allowing anyone to serve in any capacity because that idea diminishes the need for membership. A couple of good books on the subject of church membership are: *Those Who Must Give an Account: A Study of Church Membership and Church Discipline* by John Hammett and Benjamin Merkle,[54] and *Church Membership: How the World Knows Who Represents Jesus* by Jonathan Leeman and Michael Horton.[55] Both of these books offer a good study on the biblical requirements for membership and how that membership applies in the community of faith. With those who do require membership, ask this question, "If a person can serve, take Communion, participate, and lead without any qualifications or requirements, what is the purpose of membership?" Therefore, it behooves the pastor of a membership church to determine those areas of service that are permissible and those that are not.

I would highly encourage finding some areas for nonmembers to serve. Since the assimilation process begins even before a person joins the church, serving adds to that connection strength. Find ways to allow people to serve in ministries that involve a number of people in a service project. Some churches do not allow people to serve on specific teams or as ministry leaders. They also cannot teach in Sunday school. They can serve through servant evangelism projects and by joining a Sunday school class and participating in that class's service projects. Those opportunities allow nonmembers to be personally engaged with others who are church members, gaining confidence in what it means to be a Christian and a church member. The fact that the service project involves many people prevents any problems occurring because of one individual. The same idea holds true with joining a choir or a Sunday school class itself.

Every church needs to determine those parameters, realizing that they must have a balance between biblical integrity and a passion to reach the unchurched. Too much compromise may lead to a collapse of the church structure. Too much legalism may lead to the death of the church. Therefore, lead the church to the best possible scenario for that church. Do not worry what someone else does. Focus and do what the church needs.

Conclusion

The physical hindrances to church revitalization offer some important challenges for the church, but many are easily resolved. Sometimes because of financial strains, churches do not believe that they can make any improvements to themselves. The pastor offers a genuine source of encouragement at this point. Remind the people who they are in Christ. Challenge them with small projects and celebrate each time the project is completed. Remember that the Enemy uses discouragement as a primary tool for defeating believers, especially those in churches that are in decline.

As the church begins a turnaround, even if these things are quite small, the victories speak volumes to the community and to those who do not know Christ. Sometimes a fresh coat of paint, as simple as that action may be, can show those who have lost hope that some people have not given up yet. So fix the fixable and applaud the victories. Physical barriers can be overcome.

CHAPTER

6

Gifts Do Not Match the Church

I remember being in a conference listening to Bill Hybels. He recounted a question that he had been asked and was actually, at that time, asked quite often: "Are there any born leaders?" His response was, "Yes, they are all born."

His point was that leadership, while there are some who are more naturally gifted toward this characteristic, is something that can be developed. Being a naturally born leader may not be on every pastor's résumé, but every pastor can learn how to become a more effective leader. When a void exists in leadership abilities or when a clash in leadership styles occurs, the church suffers.

Leadership Ability That Does Not Match the Church

The role of the pastor is an interesting one. One of the questions I frequently encounter is, "When do I know when I should leave a church?" Obviously, that question is not only multifaceted in the question itself but also in the answer. One place where the pastor must look for the answer comes from his own leadership capabilities and the current status of the church. Most pastors would like to think that they could stay at a church for however long they like or that they could lead any size church in any situation. For some, those ideas might be true. For most in ministry, they are not.

Because of spiritual gifting, personal abilities, likes and dislikes, and backgrounds, not every pastor has the potential of success in every church. Let me give you an example. I had a young man on staff with me some years ago who was greatly talented. He was good at leading the ministry he oversaw from a teaching standpoint. His problems, though, came from the more internal issues in the church. For instance:

- He did not like staff meetings. On a multiple staff, getting together for communication and planning is essential. He was bored with these meetings, especially when something besides his ministry was being discussed.
- He did not like being one of the low men on the proverbial totem pole. At the time, our staff was built on a multitiered hierarchy based upon the size of the staff and the various ministries involved. He wanted direct access to and supervision by the lead pastor, an idea that just was not feasible at the time.
- He was not a team player. He did not like having to cooperate with other staff within his own ministry, much less with those from other ministries.
- He did not like the work requirements. Leading a ministry the size that he inherited demanded more time than what he really wanted to give. This perspective not only applied to his work-week, but also to the additional conferences, trips, and camps his ministry required. His wife felt the same way. She wanted her husband home every night by 5:00 p.m. and not gone on any trips.
- He struggled with the administrative demands of his position. Planning, cooperation, working with a host of others, and more planning all played a role of pressure in leading this ministry.

The list could go one, but the bottom line was, his gifting, likes and dislikes, and personal goals did not match the church at that time. Eventually he left for another church, one that I believe fits his abilities far better than our church did. We remain friends to this day, and I am thankful that he serves at a place that matches his leadership abilities.

From our church's perspective, the ministry suffered under his tenure, not because he was a bad person or a bad pastor, but because his abilities did not suit the current situation.

The Church at Ephesus

The Scriptures give a good perspective on leadership, length of tenure, and personal calling. The church at Ephesus most probably was a second-generation church, having had the gospel brought to the city by Aquila and Priscilla, who had been left there by Paul on his second missionary journey (see Acts 18:18–26). Paul preached there but left this couple in the city in order to plant the church. These events occurred somewhere around AD 52.

On his third missionary journey (Acts 19), Paul returned to Ephesus to further establish this fledgling congregation and pastored the church for three years, sometime between late AD 54 to early AD 57. Paul would eventually leave the city over a dispute with Demetrius the silversmith, Paul's preaching against idols, and the ensuing riot (Acts 19:24–40). He would return to Ephesus one last time after his first Roman imprisonment (AD 61–63). At this juncture, he would leave Timothy in Ephesus to pastor the church. Several problems including false doctrine (1 Tim. 1:3–7), worship disorder (1 Tim. 2:1–15), unqualified leadership (3:1–14), and materialism (6:6–19) had arisen within the congregation. Timothy was charged with the task of dealing with these issues and would remain in Ephesus at least eighteen months.[56]

Although no biblical evidence exists to prove this idea, it is thought that John the apostle spent his last days in Ephesus. Irenaeus, in his book *Against Heresies*, mentions the presence of John in Ephesus and "remaining among them permanently until the times of Trajan."[57] John most probably completed the writing of his gospel and epistles while there.[58]

The Ephesian church represents the complete stages of a congregation: planting, growing, stagnation, and dying. No one individual pastored the church throughout its entire existence. Prior to Timothy's tenure, it obviously had reached a point of stagnation and was in need of revitalization. Though it survived for several decades and is mentioned in Revelation 2:1–7, the church became known as the church that had lost its first love. John MacArthur notes,

*one who abandons
what they believed*

Irenaeus writes that Nicolas, who was made a deacon in Acts 6, was a false believer who later became an apostate; but because of his credentials he was able to lead the church astray. . . . Clement of Alexandria says, "They abandoned themselves to pleasure like goats, leading a life of self-indulgence." Their teaching perverted grace and replaced liberty with license.[59]

How does a person know when it is time to leave? Part of the answer comes from effectiveness and leadership. As difficult as it is to admit this idea, not every pastor is cut out for church revitalization. Other pastors are able to take churches to a certain level but are unable to take them beyond a particular phase of growth. Those ideas should also be considered when interviewing for a church or when the church has fallen into stagnation or decline. Stubbornness probably defines most pastors. They are not quitters and will not give up on the church. Therefore, they may stay out of loyalty or commitment, not realizing that their tenure is actually keeping the church from growing and revitalizing.

The Pastor's Assessment

Here are some questions that every pastor needs to ask in leading the church:[60]

1. **Am I the right person to lead this church?** Sometimes, as difficult as it is to admit, not everyone is equipped, geared for, or able to lead a particular church at a particular time. The pastor's age, experience, education, family circumstances, or personal walk with Christ all play into this equation. Both the prospective pastor and the established pastor need to assess these situations before trying to lead a church.
2. **Can I make the cultural adjustment to this congregation and community?** A prospective pastor has to look beyond the excitement and desire to pastor a church. The fact is, he may not be able to make the adjustment necessary to succeed and to lead change in a particular culture.
3. **Could I be a more effective leader in another church context?** I am not going to be so naïve to believe that every time someone

changes churches success results. One of the key factors already mentioned for bringing about change is longevity in the pastor's tenure. I am also not suggesting that each circumstance that brings about difficulty necessitates leaving the church. If that idea was the case, no one would stay more than eighteen months at any one congregation, if that long. Yet, one must consider that, if personal effectiveness has waned, it might be better for both the church and the pastor to consider a move.

4. **What type of church should I be leading?** Within this question comes theology, location, size, and direction. None of these issues are deal killers. For example, a part of the revitalization process might be in leading the church to become more biblical and missional in its theology. On the other hand, a church may follow orthodoxy but not orthopraxy. These ideas represent both necessary changes but also possible reasons for why the church has declined. Some resistance to change happens because the pastor tries to take the church where it does not want to go. This level of resistance can be extremely frustrating. At this point, the pastor has to know what kind of church best fits his skill set and goals. He must also ask the question if he is willing to invest the time necessary to make these changes come about.

An interesting dynamic exists in determining how long a pastor should stay at one particular church. One cannot be effective without staying long enough. At the same time, one must be wise enough to know not to stay too long. No equation exists to make those distinctions, but the pastor must be willing to ask the hard questions about effectiveness, gifting, and passion within a particular congregation. The guiding principle needs to be God's direction and a willingness to understand that a lack of results in one place does not necessarily mean failure in ministry. Pastors must be willing to admit that sometimes churches have fallen into decline because they have had a pastor who stayed too long and was ineffective for a long period of time. Other churches have declined because they have never had a pastor to stay long enough to initiate change. To be effective, one must find the balance between the two.

Staff Assessments

In addition to the pastor determining his own effectiveness in a particular congregation, questions must be asked with regard to the pastoral staff. In evaluating staff members, both paid and volunteer, one must consider gifting, effectiveness, and potential. Some staff members are presently B-team players. The challenge comes in helping them to become A-team players.

Probably one of the most popular books that addresses these issues is *Good to Great* by Jim Collins. The book applies primarily to business situations, and Collins has written some follow-up books since this one's publication, but it still offers some excellent insight into leadership structures and team evaluative measures.

Collins breaks down leadership into five categories, from the Level 1 leader to the top-tiered, Level 5 leader.[61] Here is how he develops this leadership model.

Level 5: Executive

Builds enduring greatness through a paradoxical combination of personal humility plus professional will.

Level 4: Effective Leader

Catalyzes commitment to and vigorous pursuit of a clear and compelling vision; stimulates the group to high performance standards.

Level 3: Competent Manager

Organizes people and resources toward the effective and efficient pursuit of predetermined objectives.

Level 2: Contributing Team Member

Contributes to the achievement of group objectives; works effectively with others in a group setting.

Level 1: Highly Capable Individual

Makes productive contributions through talent, knowledge, skills, and good work habits.

Part of the understanding of this leadership model, though, develops out of how each of these levels of leadership fit together. Collins suggests that the more important strategy with staff derives with asking first, "Who should be on the bus?" rather than "Where is the bus going?" In other words, when it comes to staff, change, and revitalization, it is important that the right people are in the right places first. Once people are in the right places, then the direction of the church can be determined.[62] *lack*

One of the hard facts of church life is that, with a dearth of leadership, pastors sometimes end up settling for leaders rather than waiting for the right person to come along. Sometimes waiting in the church world is not an option. No one else is available, therefore someone has to fill this spot. Multiply that scenario by months and years, and one can understand how churches get into some of the trouble in which they find themselves. The pastor must assess these situations and determine:

- Who should be on the staff?
- What position should that person hold?
- Who does not need to be on the staff?

The questions may be much easier to answer than the implementation of these answers. At this juncture, churches operate much different than businesses. Here are some ideas that must be considered:

- What is the calling of this person?
- Who will be affected by this person's change in position or departure?
- What is gained or lost in making this decision?

A cliché that must be considered when making changes is this one: *Know which hills are worth dying on.* Both paid and volunteer staff members endear themselves to their affinity groups. Unfortunately, I have seen where a staff member was so beloved that those who worked with that person did not care about his moral or ethical behavior. They loved him and were unwilling to allow this person to be removed for any reason.

That scenario can be multiplied through many church situations, and it exemplifies why church revitalization is such a difficult but necessary process.

Pat MacMillan offers some hope at this point, not for retaining the unethical staff member, but for moving people up the ladder of leadership effectiveness. He uses the dire circumstances of United Flight 232 as an example for how teams can overcome catastrophic events. He writes,

> At 37,000 feet, one hour and seven minutes out of Denver, the No. 2 engine literally broke apart. Over 70 pieces of shrapnel ripped throught the skin of the aircraft at high velocity. The heavy plane was virtually unflyable. Captain Al Haynes later described the scope of the damage: "With no hydraulics we had no ailerons to bank the airplane. We had no rudders to turn it. We had no elevators to control the pitch (that is, nose of the plane up or down) of the aircraft. We had no spoilers that come up on top of the wing to help us descend or to slow down on the ground. And, once on the ground, we would have no way to steer the plane to keep it on the runway, and no brakes to stop."[63]

One might see the church in need of revitalization like a disabled plane. In fact, an interesting response by the president of United came when asked why the company had not developed any procedures for such a predicament. He responded, "We don't have a procedure for how to fly the plane if a wing falls off either."[64] Christ did not intend for the church to stagnate and decline. Those things are not in the procedures, but it happens.

Sometimes the church crashes because the pastors do not match the church's current status. If nothing changes, a catastrophe is about to take place. MacMillan suggests that a team can overcome the impossible by developing certain characteristics. I believe these ideas will also help to move people who may need to be off the bus to a position that allows them to stay. Quoting MacMillan, the six characteristics of a high-performance team and their description include:

1. **A Clear, Common Purpose.** This [idea] serves as the cornerstone of a team. Purpose asks the question: "Why are we in existence?" Teamwork is not an end in inself, but rather a means to an end.

By definition there must be unity of purpose; otherwise, the various elements will pull in different directions. An effective team is purpose/misson-directed. It will be judged against its results.

2. **Crystal Clear Roles.** Driving the task is breaking it down and matching its various elements to corresponding strengths and skills of the various individual team members. This process becomes the key to tapping the synergystic potential of the team. Division of labor brings leverage into the equation, introducing the possibility of synergyism.

3. **Accepted Leadership.** Effective teams are characterized by clear, formal, strong leadership. Although formal leadership is clearly present at all times, an effective leader in a team environment knows that it is often best for moment-by-moment leadership to be task-driven, with significant contribution by the team member whose skills, strengths, or experience best match the demands of the current situation.

4. **Effective Processes.** Purpose deals with *what* and *why*. Here we focus on *how*. How do we accomplish the task? What are the basic processes of the team? How do we make decisions, solve problems, resolve conflict?

5. **Solid Relationships.** Interpersonal conflicts on a team are like friction in a machine. Solid relationships are the lubricant among the human beings who make up a high-performance team. The objective is not to become best friends, but to learn how to work together. The quality "solid" implies that the relationship can withstand the blows of occasional misunderstandings, conflicts, and "bad days." It is also important that individual team members feel a relationship with "the team" as well.

6. **Excellent Communication.** This one element permeates every other characteristic of an effective team. Communication provides the means of cooperation—the glue that holds the team together. Through excellent communication, we coordinate our team by assigning roles, providing feedback, clarifying details, and resolving conflicts.[65]

Staff evaluation and personal evaluation serve as two important tasks of the pastor. Both of these responsibilities become difficult, especially in the context of building relationships and teamwork. I am often asked about having and being friends on staff. These questions also have no pat answer. Somes staffs can be close friends and serve well together. Others cannot. In my opinion, the answer lies in personal integrity and calling. Church staffs should be totally different from the normal business relationships because the people on staff should be God-called to serve, and they should emulate the integrity of Christ.

In light of those thoughts, though, evaluative measures must still be in place. The following list offers an extensive questionnaire relating to staff evaluations. Each staff member should answer these questions, along with the immediate supervisor. A key element of positive reinforcement in evaluation is using terms like "achievements" and "challenges" rather than a Liekert scale of 1 to 5, with the resulting answers of "does not meet expectations" to "exceeds expectations." The pastor evaluates the staff. How the pastor receives feedback from his evaluation can be achieved through several measures. The first possibility comes from allowing other staff members to conduct his evaluation. On a small staff this process would probably be unproductive. The second way to evaluate the pastor would be through lay leadership. This process could be potentially dangerous, especially early in a pastor's ministry. It takes a few years to know who would be trustworthy with this kind of information. Some churches already have steps in place through the personnel committee. Personally, I think it places the role of the pastor as more of a hired hand than as a God-called individual. A third alternative would be to allow other pastors to conduct the evaluation. This idea works well with pastors with whom there is a long-term relationship. It probably would not be advantageous with individuals with whom there exists a cursory affiliation.

Staff Goals and Evaluation: Achievement Versus Challenge

Performance

While performance should not be the only criteria for the effectiveness of one's ministry, it certainly plays a role in church revitalization. If a person's ministry is declining, it must be noted. Extenuating circumstances might exist, but the staff needs to see if their gifts and abilities match that of the church at its present state.

- Goals set and achieved
- Strategy for reaching those goals
- Hours worked: minimum vs. maximum
- Witness: Who did you win to Christ outside of church contacts?

Teamwork

In order for a church to grow, people have to be able to work together as a unit, not as individual artists. This evaluative measure demonstrates a person's ability to see the bigger picture.

- How successful did you make others?
- Support of others' work and ministry and your attitude toward it
- Commitment to the denomination
- Support for your Team Leader and others

Loyalty

This quality is, perhaps, the most important of the entire form. There are many flaws that can be overcome, but disloyalty destroys the team. When situations become difficult in the church and people are not happy, one of the few places of solace comes from the church staff. A disloyal staff member, whether a pastor, lay leader, or secretary (ministry assistant), becomes such a hindrance that little possibility exists for church revitalization.

- Do you speak well of others on staff in public and private?
- Do you defend others when they are criticized?

Commitment

There comes a point in ministry that a commitment to one's call has to override how much money a person makes. Some staff get so caught up in salaries, days off, benefits, and worrying about how much money everyone else makes that they end up being ineffective. The church must take care of its pastors (1 Tim. 5:17–18). The pastor must protect and seek adequate provision for his staff. If money and time off serve as the priority of any staff member, senior pastor included, the church will struggle with revitalization. Sometimes during the revitalization process, the staff has to forego raises in order to have money for ministry. Are current staff cut out for that type of sacrifice?

- Ministry vs. money
- Time
- Sacrifice
- Calling
- Accountability
- Future drive vs. Squatter's rights
- What are you leaving behind?
- Vision

Leadership

Leaders can be developed, and if someone wants to lead a particular ministry, leadership qualities have to be demonstrated. Some individuals are just not ready to lead independently. Some people are better suited in direct supervision, a position that might not be possible in a particular church setting. Some do not like supervision at all, meaning that they probably need to serve elsewhere.

- Ongoing training
- Personal growth as evidenced in volunteers
- Development of new leaders
- What is my authority? (Do I have to invoke the name of someone else?)

Spiritual Development

The church will never grow beyond a pastor's personal, spiritual growth. In most cases, the church will not pray more, witness more, grow more, or love more than the pastor who leads them. Therefore, spiritual development becomes a nonnegotiable in church revitalization.

- Integrity
- Prayer life
- Bible study
- Holiness—purity
- Reputation

- Lifestyle that shows your faith
- Family life (Not just time, but are you the spiritual leader of your family and ministry?)

While this evaluation form is quite extensive and will take some time to complete, it will be extremely helpful in church revitalization, especially in determining if someone is at the right stage of ministry to be able to serve on a revitalization team. The questions or statements are intended to help the staff member work through the mental processes necessary to make an intelligent decision regarding where he/she should be serving. Some staff might realize that they have been hanging onto something that they really do not want. The evaluation will also assist the senior pastor in moving a B-team player to become an A-team player or go join another team altogether.

Conclusion

This step for many pastors reveals some of the most difficult and challenging parts of church revitalization because it involves real people. It is one thing to end a program; it is entirely another thing to remove a person. That decision affects a person's ministry, family, and walk with God. Therefore, be careful at this stage in church revitalization.

One must realize that pastors and staff can be the greatest hindrances in church revitalization, especially if gifting, talents, and abilities do not match. The pastor has to decide for himself if he possesses the necessary talents and endurance to tackle the problem of church revitalization. Those who work in ministry areas must also make these same determinations. To discover that one is not suited for a particular church is not a defeat. It takes far more courage to admit that deficiencies and a lack of passion exist than to keep leading a church into decline and eventual death. Therefore, regardless of personal friendships and personalities, one must take into consideration these qualifications and qualities; and when the hard decisions have to be made, the pastor-leader makes them with grace, mercy, love, and compassion.

CHAPTER

7

Community Demographics Differ from the Church

One of the obvious reasons for church decline and resultant revitalization stems from the fact that communities change over time. As houses age, as schools change, and as people move away, oftentimes within a matter of just a few years, the area surrounding the church can look significantly different from the church itself. Those within the church will sometimes ignore these changes and even rebel against them. Some members may resent the changes taking place and "hunker down" within the four walls of the church building. The community may have changed, but any changes that happen in the church will be over their dead bodies. Do you remember Fred the Penguin? In his meeting with the head penguins, he was told adamantly, "The iceberg is not melting!!"[66] The iceberg of twenty-year-old demographics has already melted away, but people still think that the neighborhood looks the same.

This obstacle can become one of the most devastating issues that the church faces because, at this point, it involves people, personalities, and the past. Therefore, a pastor needs to be aware of not just the demographic shifts happening in the area but also of the attitudes the church maintains because of these changes.

One of the churches that I served offers insight into this dilemma. It was a church in an area that had shown some decline, but it was not rapid . . . yet. I will say that I have not had a clearer calling to a particular church than this one. Within the next two to three years upon arriving, a precipitous change in the community occurred. In this short time frame, and in the immediate years to come, church members sold their homes and moved well beyond the suburbs to the small towns north of the city. Many continued to attend worship at the church, but the challenges increased with each passing year. I put together a Strategic Planning Committee that met for months, but many within the congregation did not receive their recommendations well. Such is the reaction to change.

Assessment

In order to understand the present state of the church and to see the direction that the community is taking, it is important to do a demographic assessment. The demographics involve both the church in question and the surrounding community.

Church Assessment

First, examine the church rolls. Include information from the following categories.

Location of Where Church Members Live. On a map, plot out where the active and inactive members live. It would be wise to distinguish between the two because the distinction may give insight into reasons for the inactivity of some members. They no longer attend because they have moved away or they no longer reflect the demographic of the community.

Age of Membership. Map out the age of active members. Find the median age of the church and of the leadership of the church. Discouragement occurs when leaders or participants are hard to find. An age evaluation may give some insight into these difficulties.

Marital Status. List the number of people who are married, divorced, widowed, or never married. This information will be critical when looking at the community at large. It also provides assistance when thinking of ministries and preaching.

Income. What is the median income of the congregation? This information will probably be the most difficult to acquire. An option that many people will find palatable is to distribute an anonymous survey to the congregation on a Sunday morning. Provide adequate explanation for the necessity of this information and its usage. This one simple action will make available most of the data that pertains to age, address, family, income, and education. Church people do react differently to new ideas, so do not get discouraged if the reaction is a resounding "NO." An alternative would be to acquire an anonymous listing of the giving records and compare those with the income levels of the community and the surrounding areas. This listing would also demonstrate the giving practices of the congregation, showing how many family units give and how often. That information is also helpful in church revitalization.

Education. Seek to determine the educational level of the congregation. This information will help in comparing the church to the community and will possibly show some of the barriers that prevent the church from reaching those who do not attend. Obviously, if the two levels do not match, the physical differences cannot be reconciled. The same idea holds true when comparing the pastor's education with the congregation's educational levels. In many cases, the pastor will be far more educated than the congregation or the community, and that education sometimes hinders the ability to lead the church. The information becomes helpful, though, in leading the church to understand that barriers exist.

Second, look for secondary demographic information that is available if good records have been kept with regard to church activity and outreach. This data includes:

How Many Small Groups Does the Church Have, Where Do They Meet, and What Is Their Purpose? Since a small group (Sunday school) offers one of the primary means of retaining and assimilating people, one can discover the perspective the church holds toward the community by examining the various small groups that meet within the church. Do they reach out to those outside of their small group? Have any of them grown in the last two to three years? Are any groups specifically focused on reaching the community?

How Many New People Have Visited the Church over the Last Year to Two Years? Of those that have visited, how many have gotten

involved in regular worship attendance or a small group? If any have
joined, how many have connected with the Sunday school?

As already mentioned on several occasions, Sunday school and small
groups offer simple ways for nonmembers to get connected with the
church. If these small groups become static or introverted, the ability to
reach the community diminishes. This issue probably reflects the bigger
problem of the church being significantly different from the surrounding
community. Think about these two ideas:

1. Healthy church growth requires new groups to start every year.
   In strong churches, about 20% of the Sunday school classes have
   been started over the previous two years. New groups have a
   greater potential to reach new people than existing groups.
2. Most existing groups lose their ability to reach new people within
   two years of starting. The difference between a growing church
   and a non-growing church is not in the number of visitors per
   week. The difference occurs in how many newcomers continue
   to attend after the first visit and how many get connected with
   a small group.

*What Has Been the Prevailing Attitude of the Church Regarding
Growth, the Community, and Change?* One can discover the answer to
these questions by reading through both the business meeting and committee meeting minutes over the last several years. Not all records will
have meticulous details of discussions that occurred, but one can possibly
glean the general perspective of the church's mind-set regarding outreach
by reading how the church responded to new ideas or change.

In interviewing church members or even the pastor search committee, rarely will a prospective pastor hear the real attitude that the church
has toward the community. No one wants to admit that the church,
not only no longer reflects the community, but it really does not want
the community to be a part of the church. This idea all falls within the
framework of church stakeholders. For example, in the church I served
that had experienced a dramatic change in demographics and had begun
to move into a self-preservation mode, most members would not have
openly expressed this attitude of resistance. It was present, however, in
meetings and in discussions about outreach and change. Revitalization

demands assessment of the church and the church's attitudes toward the community.

Community Assessment

Various forms of help are available in discovering the community dynamics and changes. One can find this data through a variety of sources.

- The United States Census. The Census Bureau provides general information regarding age, income, education, race, ethnicity, and population. The smallest demographic deals with cities, but the information gives a general understanding of changes within the area.
- The Leavell Center for Evangelism and Church Health.[67] This ministry customizes demographic studies for churches. Their work is far more specialized than the general census information.
- Glenmary Research Center.[68] This organization provides statistical data with regard to local church memberships and population trends toward church attendance. The importance of the material comes in representing the number of religious bodies located in a particular town and in giving comparative numbers for those who do not attend any religious service. Though not specific enough for a particular part of a city, the information still provides value in helping a church recognize its need and potential.
- The Chamber of Commerce
- Local Realtors
- County Planning Department

This information is useful during the process of leading the church through change. People need to understand that challenges exist. Like any data, demographics do not give the entire picture. A church can be located in the best of areas, perfectly match the community, and still not grow. The demographics provide external evidences. It will not show internal issues. It will reveal some of the reasons for these internal attitudes and will offer help for discussion starters regarding change.

Conclusion

John Kotter's metaphor offers some helpful information in learning how to bring about change, especially when people cannot quite see the external issues. He provides an eight-step process for successful change.

1. Create a sense of urgency. In the case of a melting iceberg, one must demonstrate why change is necessary and show the importance of acting immediately. Demographics can be useful at this point.
2. Pull together the guiding team. In the church, this team might be the church council, deacons, strategic planning committee, or a combination of leaders from both the staff and church. The group should be strong enough to guide the necessary changes. Qualities needed include leadership skills, integrity, good communication, analytical skills, and a sense of urgency.
3. Develop the change vision and strategy. The new team needs to clarify how these changes will help the church look different in the future from its past. It also must give insight into how these changes and the resulting future can become a reality.
4. Communicate for understanding and buy in. When it is appropriate, share this information with as many others as possible. Help them to understand the changes and to accept the new vision and strategy.
5. Empower others to act. Work through existing barriers so that the vision can succeed as planned. In the church, this process becomes difficult because it will be at this point that some will leave the church. They do not want to embrace the changes and will increase opposition.
6. Produce short-term wins. People need to see positive results from the initiated changes. Share these successes as they are accomplished.
7. Do not let up. Once the church experiences success through change, continue to initiate the changes until the vision is accomplished.
8. Create a new culture. Continue to admonish the church about the attitude changes that have occurred regarding the

community. Encourage congregants never to go back to old attitudes or mindsets, with the eventual hope that these changes become strong enough to create a new way of thinking for the church.[69]

Changing people's attitudes toward others is essentially a spiritual issue, as are many of the other revitalization issues. The pastor can preach sermons, launch committees, do the due diligence of demographic study, demonstrate clearly the lostness of the city, and people may still resist change. The reason is not because the pastor has failed in providing the necessary resources for educating the church about the needs of the community. It is simply a spiritual issue. In chapter 13, I will be talking about developing an effective prayer ministry. That section will be critical when the church rejects the community.

At this point, the pastor must resolve to stick with the congregation in spite of the spiritual battles. Running from a church in decline because the people are spiritually deficient solves nothing. The church will continue to spiral downward and the pastor goes to another church that has its own set of spiritual issues.

CHAPTER

8

The Church Turns Inward

Many times because of some of the problems and issues mentioned in the earlier chapters, a church turns inward. Leaders move into a protective mode and a resistance to change because of an innate fear of death. They will protect the church at all costs. This introversion, however, is also found in many other churches that do not face issues such as community change or any other real threat to the future of the church. They turn inward because they have lost sight of the biblical purpose of the church.

This problem demonstrates that church revitalization is necessary for many established churches, not just for those that are "dying." The issue speaks to the fact that many churches in need of revitalization do not even recognize their poverty because everything seems to be well. Examine the church at Sardis. Jesus declares, "I know your works; you have a reputation for being alive, but you are dead" (Rev. 3:1). Sardis was located forty miles southeast of Thyatira and was a rival to cities such as Smyrna and Ephesus. It was a wealthy city, with resources of gold from the river Pactolus.[70] Concerning Christ's consternation for this church, G. K. Beale writes,

> Just as the city in general was living off a former but no longer existing fame, so the same attitude had infected the church.

Though it considered itself spiritually alive, and perhaps other churches in the region respected the Sardian Christians, in reality, they were in a condition of spiritual death (cf. other such uses of "dead" in the NT). Verse 2 reveals that this assessment of their condition is a figurative overstatement (hyperbole) intended to emphasize the church's precarious spiritual state and the imminent danger of its genuine death.[71]

This description fits many churches well. They think that they are alive because attendance remains stable and finances nearly meet budget. They ignore indications that trouble is brewing and the future does not look as bright as one might imagine. The church does not realize that it has turned inward and that introversion will eventually lead the church to experience a slow leak in attendance, finances, and future.

Internal Conflicts

One of the primary reasons that a church turns inward comes from present or past conflicts within the congregation. Conflict occurs not only in the established church but also in the church plant, the church restart, and the church satellite campus. Churches have problems because people have problems, but it is for that reason that the church exists.

One of my students planted a church a few years ago. The church was growing and doing some very good ministry. I asked him in class if the church was experiencing any resistance to change. He planted the church with the mind-set of embracing change. When I asked him that question, he smiled and said, "Yes." The leadership team desired to move the worship to contain more theological depth, especially in the music. When they presented the idea to the worship team, they responded with heavy resistance. At the time, the church was only seven years old. Problems and conflicts occur in all churches of all sizes.

What happens in many situations when problems arise is that the church goes underground. Oftentimes these problems do not surface in conversations with a prospective pastor. It is why a potential pastor needs to ask specific and hard questions during the interview process. We look at demographics, location, and other physical issues with regard to the potential of the church, but even though all of those things are fixed, the church still remains in a state of decline.

Ignore It and It Will Go Away

When internal conflict arises, more times than not the church either ignores the problem or pretends that the problem does not exist. I had a church leader tell me that, even though internal conflict filled his church with power struggles, spiritual lethargy, and immorality, his church (and he emphasized the "his") did not have these problems. It was a clear state of denial. If we ignore the problem, it will go away. Unfortunately, that hope rarely if ever becomes a reality.

The church at Corinth tried this same solution. Immorality was rampant in the congregation, and the church just ignored what was going on. The church was embroiled in constant conflict. Paul wrote, "For it has been reported to me about you, my brothers, by members of Chloe's household, that there is rivalry among you" (1 Cor. 1:11). In other words, power struggles and leadership issues stood at the forefront of this church's problems. Because of bad leadership, moral compromise occurred (1 Cor. 5:9–13), unbiblical behavior became rampant (1 Cor. 6:1–11), and immorality increased (1 Cor. 6:12–20), among other things. Internal conflict and a lack of spiritual growth manifested themselves into physical realities. The church at Corinth just decided to ignore these problems, both external and internal. The modern church usually follows the same procedure. The church ignores internal conflict, and that reason alone causes the church to fall into decline.

Unforgiveness and the Root of Bitterness

Unforgiveness represents the foremost internal conflict most often ignored in the church. For some reason, the church expects members to follow Scripture except when it comes to personal relationships within the body. We must be biblical unless kindness and forgiveness are involved. We believe in biblical fidelity until we go into a business meeting or write on our blogs. In these two cases, the Bible's call to be "kind and compassionate to one another, forgiving one another, just as God also forgave you in Christ" (Eph. 4:32) falls on deaf ears. I am amazed at some Christians who are highly critical of the church yet never recognize their own transgressions in the ugly things they write about other Christians or the church. Those who live in glass houses. . . .

The reality is that Christians struggle with other Christians in the church. Sometimes their struggles are authentic. Another person has genuinely hurt them and has not sought reconciliation. Sometimes the problems exist because of personal selfishness or pride. That person would not do what I wanted him/her to do. Other times, people bring baggage with them from other failed relationships and refuse to give anyone new a chance. Regardless of the reasons, when church members carry unforgiveness in their hearts, that unforgiveness eventually turns into a bitterness that affects the entire congregation. Everyone knows that something is wrong, but no one seems to be able to identify it exactly.

Added to the internal conflicts caused by church members is the bitterness generated by and sometimes modeled by the pastor. Because of pastoral failure and even success, church members respond with unresolved anger and uncertainty. The pastor who accepts the church's call, only to stay until a larger congregation comes along (even sending out résumés before the chair is warm in the pastor's office), can leave people with almost as much of a sour outlook on pastoral ministry as if unrepentant, moral failure had occurred.

Couple this tragedy with the unforgiveness pastors develop because of how they have been treated by other churches and Christians. Though no one wants to admit it, a tremendous amount of anger exists in many pastors' hearts. They know it is sin, but it becomes much easier to ignore it, spiritualize it, or justify it rather than eradicate it from their lives. That internal conflict radiates in how pastors treat and respond to church members, with bitterness and anger resulting from both parties.

Hebrews speaks of this dilemma. The writer admonishes, "Pursue peace with everyone, and holiness—without it no one will see the Lord. Make sure that no one falls short of the grace of God and that no root of bitterness springs up, causing trouble and by it, defiling many" (Heb. 12:14–15). That root of bitterness, whether it lives in the heart of the church or the pastor or both, ends up quenching God's Spirit and causing the church to fall into decay.

Fix the Problem or Die

In both the Old and New Testaments, two foundational principles provide the basis for God's forgiveness. First, God desires that all humanity be in fellowship with Him and know Him. Second, all human beings are sinners separated from God who cannot restore that fellowship on their own. Forgiveness is necessary and possible because of God's work.[72]

One can find at least eight specific words that communicate the idea of forgiveness in the Bible. Four are found in the Old Testament and four in the New.

The Old Testament Words for Forgiveness

The four main words in the Old Testament include:

1. *Salach:* to send away. A familiar passage where this word appears is 2 Chronicles 7:14, where God says to Solomon that He will "hear from heaven, forgive their sin, and heal their land." The idea of the word is that God sends away the otherwise inevitable consequences, i.e., eternal separation from Him. When we are forgiven, God takes our sin and sends it away from us.

2. *Nasa:* to lift up a burden. Sin creates guilt in a person's life that becomes like a curse or a plague. Forgiveness lifts the burden off of the person. An example is the sin of Joseph's brothers who sold him into slavery. The request from Joseph's father was for Joseph to "forgive your brothers' transgression and their sin" (Gen. 50:17). When God forgives, He removes the guilt and the burden that sin causes.[73]

3. *Kaphar:* to cover, to atone. The Bible is clear that a person cannot cover sin any more than Abel could hide the murder of his brother. In Psalm 78:38, the word is used to describe how God could have destroyed Israel, "yet He was compassionate; He atoned [forgave] for their guilt." When God forgives, He covers our sin so that it cannot be seen. The Septuagint (the Greek translation of the Old Testament circa 280–100 BC) uses the Greek word *aphiemi* to translate *nasa, salach,* and *kaphar.*[74] This Greek word will be discussed in the next section.

4. *Machah:* to blot out. When a person sins, that sin leaves an indel-ible mark, a record you might say. God, though, blots out the record of sin. Isaiah records how God identified Himself to Israel as "It is I who sweep away [blot out] your transgressions for My own sake and remember your sins no more" (Isa. 43:25). When God forgives, He blots out the record of our sin so that it cannot be remembered.[75]

New Testament Words for Forgiveness

The four major New Testament words for forgiveness include:

1. *Apolyein:* to put away. It is used only once in the New Testament, Luke 6:37, "Forgive, and you will be forgiven."
2. *Paresis:* to put aside or to disregard. It is also found only once in the New Testament in Romans 3:25, "God presented Him as a propitiation through faith in His blood, to demonstrate His righteousness, because in His restraint God passed over the sins previously committed."
3. *Charizesthai:* the graciousness of God's forgiveness. It is used only by Paul to convey forgiveness of sin. Ephesians 4:32 states, "And be kind and compassionate to one another, forgiving one another, just as God also forgave you in Christ."
4. *Aphesis:* sending away, letting go. It is the most common word in the New Testament, used fifteen times as a noun and about forty times as a verb. Matthew 26:28 says, "For this is My blood that establishes the covenant; it is shed for many for the forgiveness of sins."[76]

The Biblical Requirements for Forgiveness

Many passages set for the church the biblical requirements for per-sonal forgiveness. One of the most important of these texts is 1 John 1:9. This verse establishes a very clear understanding of how people receive God's forgiveness and what that forgiveness provides.

Forgiveness Requires the Confession of Our Sin

The apostle John makes a very simple statement that sets the stage for how sins are forgiven. He says, "If we confess our sins . . ." The word *confess* literally means "to speak the same thing."[77] It infers that one must agree that personal sin exists by saying the same thing about sin that God says about sin. The act, or lack of, is probably the reason why many do not experience any release from their guilt. When dealing with someone who does not think God can forgive them, help them to understand that forgiveness starts with a person's willingness to admit that he/she has personally and specifically sinned against God and His laws.

Forgiveness Occurs because of Who God Is

John says that, within the nature of God, two characteristics exist that prove why forgiveness is possible. He writes, "He [meaning God] is faithful and righteous. . . ." For God to be faithful means that God is always trustworthy.[78] He never lets believers down. Everett R. Storms has estimated that there are 7,487 promises in the Bible that God makes to humanity.[79] In examining these promises, God has not failed to fulfill every one that was intended to be fulfilled by now. There are some promises yet to be fulfilled, but they will be within the timing of God.

God is also righteous, describing that His means of judgment are always fair.[80] God does not judge us based upon human bias. Some people think that God cannot forgive them because they have seen how people do not forgive. They say they forgive, but then they do not forget. God's forgiveness is not determined by the perspective of man but by the death of Christ on the cross. God is just in forgiving because Christ paid the price for our sins. Danny Akin explains, "God is able and righteous in forgiving because these sinners will have confessed their sins and trusted in God's revelation of eternal life in Jesus his Son, whose death is the basis for forgiveness."[81] Believers can count on God to forgive sin because of Who He is.

Forgiveness Results in the Removal of the Guilt and the Eternal Penalty of Sin

John declares that our confession of sin and God's trustworthiness result in two things. He says that God is faithful and just to "forgive us our sins and cleanse us from all unrighteousness" (1 John 1:9). The word *forgive* means "to send away." The concept originates out of the Day of Atonement in the Old Testament. The act of forgiveness was symbolized when the High Priest laid his hands on the head of the scapegoat, confessed the sins of the nation upon the goat, and then sent the goat out into the wilderness, never to return.[82] When God forgives, He removes our sin from us. It is important to remember what Paul said about what God did in Jesus, "He made the One who did not know sin to be sin for us, so that we might become the righteousness of God in Him" (2 Cor. 5:21).

God also cleanses people from sin. Where forgiveness speaks of our relationship to God, cleansing deals with the guilt and the dirt of sin. When people experience God's forgiveness, they also can forgive themselves because God removes the stain of sin. It means to be without blemish, spotless, and pure.[83] Both the words *forgive* and *cleanse* are considered to be finished works in the Greek New Testament (they are aorist tense verbs). In other words, the work of forgiveness and the removal of guilt are done and finished. When God forgives, it is not partial. He forgives completely.

Leading the Church to Forgive

First John 1:9 also provides the biblical solution for how Christians can forgive, including forgiving the pastor and the pastor forgiving the church. The two characteristics of God mentioned offer a paramount understanding into how forgiveness occurs. When one person hurts another person, the offended party struggles with forgiveness because he/she has been robbed of something, whether it is a person's dignity, reputation, self-worth, or something else. People struggle to forgive because they cannot forget. Forgiveness, though, has little to do with forgetting as much as it does with releasing—sending away. Therefore, in forgiveness, a person must claim the trustworthiness of God's character, that is, He is faithful and righteous. Faithful means that He will never let a believer down. Righteous or just indicates that God will handle the offense according to His law and His grace.

The offended party must give the hurtful words and actions to Christ. Trust that He will handle the situation exactly in a way that demonstrates Christ's love for His people. Let go of what has been taken and rest in the promises of God. Thus, forgiveness is not about forgetting or getting even; it is about releasing the hurt and trusting the Savior.

Conclusion

The internal conflicts of unforgiveness and anger are not always easily recognized. They must be addressed and removed if the church is going to survive. Unforgiveness and the resulting bitterness become recognizable attitudes, not only by church members, but also by outsiders. No one may be able to identify the problem, but people immediately sense that something is wrong with the church. A newcomer who perceives that church members do not like each other is rarely going to return. The church that gets a reputation for unforgiveness in the community essentially nails its own coffin shut. The revitalization pastor may need to set plans and changes aside first to lead the church to forgive. Once forgiveness is in place, revitalization becomes a genuine possibility.

9

External Factors

While it is possible to trace many of the problems that cause church decline to sinful behaviors or poor leadership, some issues surface that cannot be blamed on any one person, program, or committee. These issues, however, represent just as much of a threat to the church's future as do the problems created from within. They create much dismay for the revitalization pastor because it initially appears as though the church is powerless to resolve these conflicts. An awareness of them allows the church to make adjustments so that the pastor can lead them through some specific corrective steps and a reversal of the decline.

Financial Recession

During the last several decades, the United States and the world economy have suffered from several recessions. In the early 1990s, the U.S. recorded an eight-month recession that led to an increase in inflation and interest rates. Ten years later, because of the September 11, 2001 attacks on America, another recession came into play. This recession, though some analysts declared that it also only lasted eight months, had enduring effects on the economy. Between December 2007 and June 2009, the most recent recession hit the American economy again. This recession occurred as the housing market collapsed and as many of America's largest financial institutions failed, including Fannie Mae, Freddie Mac, Lehman Brothers, and AIG. Even the auto industry encountered a deep crisis. In response, the federal government provided a bailout program for both the banks and the automobile makers.[84]

When the economy suffers, the fallout affects the people of the church. Job loss, decreased salaries or benefits, and a drop in liquid assets such as stocks or property all impact the church's income. The church does not have a product to sell (though some seem to be selling Jesus at times). Finances come primarily from donations, and when a family's income drops, so do the offerings most of the time.

Corrective Steps

Recognize the Underlying Issue of Poor Financial Stewardship. The real problem is spiritual. That fact continues to surface throughout the chapters of this book. People will continue to buy toys, take multiple vacations, and eat out on a regular basis even when money is tight. The last thing they think about is the church. The revitalization pastor who serves a church in financial recession needs to evaluate the spiritual tone of the church. As already explicated, sometimes the first thing that has to happen in order for a church to revitalize is that it needs revival.

Commit to Biblical Preaching. The answer also lies in discipling people through the preaching of the Word. Do not ever underestimate the power of God's Word to change people's hearts, even when it comes to the practice of generosity. In today's church culture, there seems to be somewhat of a backlash toward the idea of tithing. Since tithing is an Old Testament law, people think that it is not a legitimate practice under grace. I will not go through a theological diatribe to defend tithing or any kind of giving as law. Giving is, however, a responsibility for believers. It is a matter of the heart. The apostle Paul gives us the New Testament mandate and mind-set for generosity. He writes,

> Remember this: The person who sows sparingly will also reap sparingly, and the person who sows generously will also reap generously. Each person should do as he has decided in his heart— not reluctantly or out of necessity, for God loves a cheerful giver. And God is able to make every grace overflow to you, so that in

every way, always having everything you need, you may excel in every good work. (2 Cor. 9:6–8)

Teach people the Word. It will change lives and hearts, even when it comes to money.

Declining Population Base

Another obstacle to growth and revitalization occurs when the area around the church begins to decline. This issue offers, perhaps, the greatest challenge to revitalization because it puts the church in a nearly losing battle.

My current church partnered with another church for a few years that faced this very situation. The church has been in a steady decline for years. Part of their demise originated from an ill-conceived vision and strategy. They wanted to be an upper-middle class white church located in a lower-middle class ethnically diverse neighborhood. At this point, the sociological makeup of the church did not match that of the neighborhood, and the church essentially rejected any idea of reaching that balance. This perspective led the church to some conflict and great decline.

By the time we arrived, the church had around fifty to seventy attendees in a sanctuary that held seven hundred. The buildings were in disrepair, a problem we sought to rectify as best we could. The greatest issue was that by now, the neighborhood had changed to where when people moved out, no one moved in. Either the banks (financial recession) or the property owners boarded up the houses and left them vacant.

Corrective Steps

Rethink Mission and Purpose. This dilemma requires the pastor and the church to rethink the purpose of their existence. It necessitates strategic planning for the future and intentional demographic study. If the church genuinely has a commitment to the community, it must research and launch creative ministries that meet the needs of the neighborhood. Although both the church and the area face financial recession, that difficulty places the church in an advantageous position.

Become an Advocate for the Neighborhood. At this point, the neighborhood needs the church. Lead the church to become an advocate for the neighborhood. Develop marketing and ministry that lets the community know that the church has not forgotten about them, nor will it abandon them. Talk with city/county officials about what the church can do to revitalize the neighborhood. When the neighborhood revitalizes, the church revitalizes.

A couple of helpful books at this point are David Platt's *Radical: Taking Back Your Faith from the American Dream*[85] and *Radical Together: Unleashing the People of God for the Purpose of God.*[86] While these books address more of the suburbanites leaving their comfort zones to reach out to those of a different socioeconomic status, the premise becomes a good model for the church that already lives this reality.

Find Partnerships with Both Neighboring Churches and Healthy, Missional Churches. In the church revitalization ministry, the barriers sometimes necessitate crossing denominational lines in order to accomplish the work. I am not suggesting compromising biblical or ethical tenets, but churches often forfeit ministry because of labels and preconceived ideas.

First, find those churches in the general area of the neighborhood that might share in the mission for the community. One of the benefits of having a revitalization pastor at a church in the declining neighborhood is vision. The pastor possesses a calling to be at that church and dreams of what that church can become. Many times in declining neighborhoods, churches do not have that kind of pastor. Therefore, the ministry of the revitalization pastor reaches both other churches and discouraged pastors.

- Partner with these churches.
- Pool resources to do community events and outreach.
- Survey the community for specific needs and strategize how to meet those needs.
- Pray together often.

Second, find healthy churches that emulate a missional ecclesiology and establish an ongoing partnership with them. Church-planting pastors find churches with whom they can partner in order to have a strong foundation even before the church launches. Do not allow the pride of the church or the pastor to keep the declining congregation from revitalizing.

- Lead the declining church to develop an Acts 1:8 strategy, understanding that a part of their role is to reach this Jerusalem.
- Discover healthy, missional churches that share that same strategy. Invite them to partner with the declining church to be a part of their Jerusalem/Judea/Samaria.
- Do not make the partnership just about money. Make it a partnership of resources, people, mission, and ministry.
- Look for like-minded pastors who have an interest in joining the declining church team for revitalization (contact other churches, colleges, and seminaries for these resources).
- Guide the church through a concert of prayer, taking an entire service to seek God's guidance, wisdom, and provision for this revitalization project.

Competition with Other Churches

No one would want to admit this fact, but churches do compete with each other for members and guests. For that reason, churches market themselves and develop ministries, programs, and strategies that allow that church to rise above the others. This competition does not just affect those churches in declining areas. It can serve as a reason for a revitalization strategy for a church that has stagnated even though it is located in a growing community.

Competition between churches is an age-old phenomenon. It did not just begin with the introduction of the contemporary church model. Churches have always competed. Additionally, some churches/pastors do not demonstrate a strong ethic when it comes to this competition. No one wants to admit that fact, but I will say it. As a pastor, I have seen other pastors manipulate, use questionable methods, and pretend to be something that they really were not. This lack of pastoral integrity gives justification for church suspicion and eventual decline.

The competition becomes heavy as churches depend more on programming or methodology than on a missional strategy. Thus, when a new church moves in the area, people compare programs, worship styles, and ministries. The analogy I use is the health club. If I am a member of a health club and a new one moves in across the street, and its equipment is better, the hours are more convenient, and the dues are the same, I am going to change my membership. A lack of brand loyalty defines many within today's church culture, and this fact clearly reveals itself when churches compete.

Corrective Steps

Lead the Church to Develop Its Own Identity. If programs and methods drive the church, competition becomes fierce and the smaller, less "cool" church loses. As a revitalization pastor, help the church find its niche in the church world. Chapter 14 explains the Change Matrix and will more deeply define how to develop this specific focus.

Be Driven by Mission Rather than by Programming. Harry Reeder explains,

> Dying churches tend to be focused on programs. Like a gambler looking for a winning ticket, they search for a program that will "turn their church around." They are pinning their hope for success on the latest organized ministry or prepackaged church-growth plan, and they evaluate the health of the church by the number and impressiveness of such programs.[87]

This challenge does not mean that the church should eliminate all programs and ministries and "just love Jesus." What should happen is that the church's mission should determine what programs it uses and what methods are valid, not the other way around. Being program-driven leads to competition because both churches have to prove who has the better program, or what I call the "dog and pony show." Missionally-driven churches know who they are and why they exist. Therefore, they mostly eliminate the pressure or need to compete. (I am not so naïve to believe that all competition ceases, because I understand the fall of humanity and the market mind-set of the world.)

Promote the Mission of the Church. Anytime, anywhere, and through any means, talk about the church's mission. Keep that mission in front of the church and in front of the world. Redirect old thoughts of programming and a self-centered ministry to a new perspective of church mission. The church exists for the community, not the community exists for the church.

Get Out and Serve the Community. Some of the other barriers in church revitalization revealed in this book share this same solution. A later chapter will further explain this idea, but service provides one answer to the program-driven quandary. Start out small and build upon the ministries and service projects that best define the church's mission.

A Community That Is Highly Resistant to the Gospel

This problem continues to be a rising issue for all churches, regardless of their size, location, or past. America is heading down a slippery slope of moral decay and biblical rejection to where the nation now has become far more resistant to the gospel than ever before. This reason, I believe, has led many churches to compromise in areas of biblical fidelity, moral stands, and methodologies. The rise in popularity in narrative preaching that only tells stories with little biblical application, the rejection of propositional truth even in preaching, and the moderation in moral absolutes all are symptoms of how churches are incorrectly trying to overcome this issue. The thought that we need to become like the world in order to reach the world permeates ecclesiological and salvific discussions. When one's church is in decline, it becomes very tempting to give into these compromises.

Thom Rainer wrote a book several years ago that addresses the very issue of a high resistance to the gospel. His research concludes of American adults:

- 5% are highly resistant to the gospel
- 21% are somewhat resistant to the gospel
- 36% are neutral
- 27% are receptive to the gospel
- 11% are highly receptive to the gospel[88]

Anecdotally, I would conclude that those numbers have changed significantly since the publication of Rainer's book. It seems as though more people are highly resistant to the gospel in today's world. It is also disturbing that 7 percent of the respondents who said that they were highly resistant to the gospel were under the age of eighteen. Only 3 percent were somewhat friendly and no percentage was recorded for any people under eighteen being highly friendly. Couple the 7 percent number with another 40 percent of those who were highly resistant to the gospel being in the nineteen to thirty-five age range, and one finds that, of those who are highly resistant to the gospel, 47 percent are thirty-five years old and under.[89]

The American Religious Identification Survey (ARIS) 2008 would justify this conclusion of an increased resistance. Their research shows:

- 76% Americans say they are Christian (2008), down from 86% in 1990. 34% of adults say they are born-again Christians
- No religion: 14.3 mil (8.2%) 1990; 29.4 mil (14.1%) 2001; 34.1 mil (15%) 2008
- Non-Christian religion: 5.8 mil (3.3%) 1990; 7.7 mil (3.7%) 2001; 8.7 mil (3.9%) 2008
- Baptists: 33.9 mil (19.3%) 1990; 33.8 mil (16.3%) 2001; 36.1 mil (15.8%) 2008
- Mainline: 32.7 mil (18.7%) 1990; 35.7 mil (17.2 %) 2001; 29.3 mil (12.9%) 2008
- Muslim: 527K (.3%) 1990; 1.1 mil (.5%) 2001; 1.3 mil (.6%) 2008[90]

This information demonstrates that mainline denominations have dropped in both numbers and in the percentage of the population. Baptists, even though they have experienced a slight increase in numbers, have dropped in their percentage representation within the adult population. Those who say that they have no religion at all offer perhaps the most disturbing of the statistics. Those figures have nearly doubled in percentage and have more than doubled in actual numbers.

Another disturbing trend comes from the age composition of the various religious traditions. Younger people are not being reached within the Christian faith as much as they are through other religions. Among Christians, 20 percent of attendees are eighteen to twenty-nine. Among Eastern Religions, the number rises to 37 percent, and among Muslims, the number surges to 42 percent.[91]

Corrective Steps

Rainer offers several observations regarding the highly resistant and some solutions to this problem.

Use Special Events. While the vast majority of those who are highly resistant to the gospel never attend a worship service, 13 percent still attend for special activities and ministries,[92] and 20 percent were somewhat likely to attend church if someone invited them.[93] Develop some creative events that address "self-help" topics, such as issues with the family or finances. Do not do a "bait and switch," where the church tells the community that one thing will happen then hits them with a weighty invitation or an overt gospel presentation. Churches are notorious for this tactic. With special events, use registration cards with a section where people can request more information on the church or the Christian life. Overwhelm them with kindness, not pressure.

Invest in Building Relationships. Most of those who are highly resistant have negative attitudes about the church and the Bible, rejecting any thought of the existence of heaven and hell. To use some form of initiative evangelism would most probably be fruitless. Rainer says that reaching the highly resistant is extremely difficult. Many of them have been deeply hurt, with 69 percent saying that they have had a negative experience with the church or with a Christian. Building genuine relationships so that the highly resistant can meet a genuine believer in real situations can overcome these negative opinions. It also challenges the church to get healthy and stay healthy. If non-Christians are having that many negative experiences with the church and with Christians, believers need to get serious about the Christian life. Of those who are highly receptive to the gospel, 97 percent recall a positive church experience.[94] Christians need to understand that their behavior toward others is an essential element in sharing the gospel.

Use Apologetics as a Witnessing Tool.[95] Reaching the highly resistant requires a greater investment in time and training than with those who are somewhat or highly receptive to the gospel. One area of training material that is fruitful is apologetics. Kenneth Boa and Robert Bowman define apologetics as "the discipline concerned with the defense of the faith . . . a general grouping of approaches or systems developed for defending the faith, as when we speak of evidential apologetics . . . [and] as an activity of presenting an apology or apologies in defense of the faith."[96] Because apologetics involves the use of reason, logic, and evidence, it can be effective in handling the objections of the highly resistant if they reject Christianity based on reason, science, or history.

A Community That Is Stable

A conclusion that pastors and churches sometimes draw is that the church cannot grow because the neighborhoods around the church have stopped growing. Therefore, many churches relocate or start new campuses. Once the surrounding community stabilizes, the church must look elsewhere for prospects.

The fact is, however, that even in a stable community, change is taking place. Some families are still moving out and new ones are replacing those who left. This situation is obviously not ideal and the church often stagnates in the midst of this transition, but the revitalization pastor must lead the church to stay focused on the Great Commission, especially in reaching the local area.

Every church must recognize that most any community is going to stabilize at some point. God only created so much land, and once that land is developed, He is not going to create any more space. Therefore, the church has to decide to either put wheels under its buildings so that it can move every time the population base stabilizes, it can forget about its current location and add additional locations to its roster, or it can realize that potential still exists in its present location. Phenomenal growth is not going to be the experience of every church. Sometimes when a church grows too fast, it actually becomes unhealthy as a result. Most churches possess the potential for steady, consistent growth, even those churches in stable communities.

Corrective Steps

Lead the Church to Understand Its Mission. When the church (or the pastor) gets discouraged, it is important to get back into the Scriptures and be reminded of the church's purpose and mission. Teach on 1 Corinthians 12, a passage that addresses the topic of spiritual gifts but also speaks to the body of Christ as a whole. Within the local church, not everyone is an eye or an ear. In the body of Christ, not every church

work w/ Chamber of Commerce

is the same. Each church has its own mission, calling, and purpose. Help the church understand the purpose for which God has chosen her.

Invest in Reaching Out to Newcomers. In a stable community, use available resources to find when a family moves out of the community and make a concerted effort to introduce the church to the new family who has moved into the area. Do not overdo it but have a welcome team that enjoys meeting new people. Work like the "Welcome Wagon" of days gone by. Put together a basket with gifts and coupons from local businesses. Offer to provide free labor to help the new family move their furniture, if the moving company does not already provide that service. Find some creative ways to welcome newcomers even before they come to church.

Serve the Community. Unless the community is unique, the neighborhood will still have people who are unreached and do not attend church. It may be that they have never attended or have been hurt in the past. They may have been somewhat resistant to the gospel in the past, but now because of changes or crises in their lives, openness exists. The church oftentimes thinks that, because they have unsuccessfully witnessed to someone previously, it is unnecessary to witness to them again. The church gives up too easily on people. Get out and serve people, and let God use that service to make people more responsive.

Use the Diversity of the Congregation for an Advantage. How does the church reflect the community? Most probably in a stable situation, the church better reflects the neighborhood than in other situations. Use that fact as an advantage. Make sure that the church's programs offer ministry to the community's needs. Make the church a community church by offering its services, buildings, and even staff to assist community efforts.

Connect with the Local Funeral Homes and Nursing Homes. Oftentimes in stable communities, there are those individuals who have never connected with the church. If the pastor and the church will make themselves available, these two industries offer an incredible number of contacts. Volunteer to conduct funerals for people who have no church connection. Develop ministries to the nursing homes, not only for the patients, but also for the employees, their families, and the families of the patients.

Conclusion

It would be nice to just open the doors of the church and see people fill the pews (or seats). Except in rare situations, that phenomenon does not happen. It takes work to revitalize a church and to get it growing again, especially when the church faces external situations beyond its control. Now the workload gets more difficult.

The revitalization pastor must commit to "be serious about everything, endure hardship, do the work of an evangelist, fulfill your ministry" (2 Tim. 4:5). Those words of Paul to the revitalization pastor named Timothy ring true for the church today. The pastor must remain faithful to the calling of God on his life. If revitalization becomes a part of that call, do not give up when circumstances become more difficult. See the obstacles as God-given challenges for the church to survive. Be creative or talk with some creative people who can help in developing corrective steps for whatever hindrances exist. Do not give up on the church until God gives up on the church. The church still belongs to Jesus!

CHAPTER

10

The Church Has Lost Its Vision

When the church experiences conflict with its pastor, its leadership, or within the church in general, oftentimes the church loses its vision. This conflict, especially when it occurs within the church leadership, leads to a loss of shared vision. Thus, the church begins to decline because it does not know where it is going.

Vision or a planned direction is essential for any organization. Burt Nanus, in his book *Visionary Leadership,* writes, "There is no more powerful engine driving an organization toward excellence and long-range success than an attractive, worthwhile, achievable vision for the future, widely shared."[97] If the church loses its vision, it loses direction and begins to decline. Church revitalization necessitates the establishment of a renewed vision with which the church can unify.

Vision Defined

Hans Finzel offers an interesting definition of vision, a rather practical statement that not only says what vision is but what it does. He writes, "A vision is a picture of the future state for the organization, a description of what it would like to be a number of years from now. It is a dynamic picture of the organization in the future, as seen by its leadership. It is more than a dream or set of hopes, because top management is demonstrably committed to its realization: it is a commitment."[98] Thus, vision

159

sets the direction of the church, giving it purpose, meaning, and a reason for its existence. To discover and communicate this purpose necessitates both a general understanding of the purpose of the body of Christ but also a specific purpose of how one particular church seeks to fulfill that vision within the context of its lifetime.

The Primary Function of the Church (The Big Picture)

In order to get the church back on track when no shared vision exists, the pastor must first lead the church to understand why Jesus created the church. It is a biblical issue at this point. Most Christians know the Great Commission expressed in Matthew. When looking at the end of Jesus' ministry here on the earth, one must take into account the last words that He spoke. Last words are important. Jesus took His disciples on a high mountain, one from which much of their known world could be seen. To the north, they could see the tip of the Sea of Galilee. To the east lay the Jordan Valley leading to Perea. Further east were the southern cities of the Decapolis, including Gadara and Gerasa. To the west, the disciples could see parts of Samaria. Finally, to the south, Jerusalem would be visible on a clear day.

Jesus then said to these men, "Go, therefore, and make disciples of all nations, baptizing them in the name of the Father and of the Son and of the Holy Spirit, teaching them to observe everything I have commanded you. And remember, I am with you always, to the end of the age" (Matt. 28:19–20). Jesus makes one command: to make disciples. The process occurs through going, baptizing, and teaching. Those ideas present the one commission Christ gives to the church, a command that is still in effect today.

When a church loses its vision, most probably the trouble traces back to a loss of understanding about the Great Commission. Sometimes it is theological. Previous pastors or laypeople may have failed to teach the real meaning of these words, and they have bought into a substitute purpose for the church. Sometimes the problem is internal. When the church experiences problems and people respond to one another in anger and unforgiveness, they forget about the Great Commission. People overlook those who do not know Christ when they are not in fellowship with one another. Finally, if that reputation spills out into the community, the church will struggle to get anyone interested in listening to its message.

The problem moves from theological to internal to pragmatic. Therefore, to get the church back on track:

- Spend time going back to the basics
- Teach and preach on the purpose of the church
- Develop short-term projects or opportunities for the church to experience and fulfill the Great Commission
- Lead the church to practice forgiveness

Ron Jenson and Jim Stephens echo this sentiment:

Rallying the members of a local church around the common objective of making disciples will have enormous implications for the growth of the church. Many churches have lost sight of their purpose. Knowing and understanding the objective gives direction and meaning to all a church does.

An awareness that outreach to the community and the world is central to its existence affects a church's quantitative growth. When a church sees itself as a base of ministry to those living around it, it will be continually praying and thinking about effective ways to minister to the community. This will be a natural preoccupation because the church exists to minister.[99]

Thus, in order for the church to revitalize, it must renew its commitment to its central function: fulfilling the Great Commission.

What Vision Is Not

Aubrey Malphurs offers assistance in understanding vision by defining what it is and what it is not. In defining vision, he writes:

A Vision Is Not a Dream. The terms may be used synonymously, but, in fact, a dream is much broader than a vision. Often the envisioning process begins with a dream. Dreams initiate or fuel visions.

A Vision Is Not Goals and Objectives. Goals and objectives are cold and abstract things that do not warm the heart. Vision, however, is warm and concrete and has the potential to melt the coldest heart. Just as a dream precedes a vision, so a vision precedes goals and objectives.

A Vision Is Not a Purpose. Most often purpose answers the question, Why? Vision answers the question, What? I argue that the purpose of the church is to glorify God (Rom. 15:6; 1 Cor. 6:20), whereas the mission and vision of the church concern the Great Commission (Matt. 28:19–20).

A Vision Is Not a Mission. A ministry's mission is a statement of where it is going; whereas, its vision is a picture or snapshot of the same. Primarily the mission affects planning the organization's future, while the vision affects the communication of that future.[100]

What a Vision Is

Malphurs also explains what comprises a vision. He personally defines vision as "a clear and challenging picture of the future of a ministry as you believe that it can and must be."[101] Within the context of this definition, Malphurs clarifies that vision must contain these six facets:

A Vision Is Clear. If the people who make up the ministry do not or cannot understand the vision, then there is no vision regardless of the amount of time spent in developing it.

A Vision Is Challenging. The problem for most ministry visions is that once they are conceived and born, they face a quick, untimely death and are quietly buried in some vision graveyard. If people are not challenged by the vision, there really is no vision.

A Vision Is a Mental Picture. A good vision probes the imagination in such a way that it conjures up visual representations in the mind. John R. W. Stott says of vision, "It is an act of seeing—an imaginative perception of things, combining insight and foresight. . . . We see what it is—but do we see what it could be?"

A Vision Is the Future of the Ministry. Vision is always cast in terms of the future. It is a mental picture of what tomorrow will look like. Most visions are perpetually in the state of becoming and thus remaining futuristic. These are long-term and open-ended visions.

A Vision Can Be. A good vision has potential. It rests firmly on the bedrock of reality—thus it is highly feasible.

A Vision Must Be. A good vision grabs hold and will not let go. Several factors contribute to this conviction:

- God is in it
- God has chosen to accomplish this vision through this particular person
- The vision will benefit people
- The visionary is also convinced that the vision must be because of his passion for that vision.[102]

These ideas provide an excellent foundation upon which a pastor can build or rebuild the vision for the church. If the church has no real direction or is divided with regard to what the church should be doing, cast vision for them. Help them to dream again.

The Vision Cycle

Part of the reason that vision becomes a problem is because of the cyclical nature of vision. The big picture of vision for the Body of Christ found in Scripture never changes, but how churches put that vision into practice adjusts as years pass, as they achieve parts of the vision, and as leadership grows, matures, or shifts. Because of these variations, churches sometimes lose sight of their vision or divide over the true definition of that vision. They fail to understand that a church's vision needs readjusting or tweaking at times. If the church has lost its vision, it needs to reenvision what God wants the church to be.

Robert Dale's book *To Dream Again* offers some excellent insight at this point. Dale writes:

> There are four ways to revitalize a church, organizationally speaking. The easiest change is policy change. You simply adjust the way you do things.
>
> A second strategy is to change personnel. Firing the minister or electing new lay leaders is a common approach.
>
> Another change tactic is to create new program structures. Reorganization plans are familiar in institutions of all kinds.

Change policy. Change people. Change programs. Each of these approaches has its advocates. But the approach I suggest is the most basic of all—clarify purpose.

The fourth way to revitalize a church is to define and act on its fundamental purpose. A new dream awakes a congregation. A poster motto challenges: "Aim for the sun. You may not reach it, but you will fly higher than if you never aimed at all."[103]

Dale then offers an excellent look at the cyclical nature of a vision. Every vision, if not revisited and restructured at times, goes through this cycle. Oftentimes the plateaued church finds itself stuck because the vision has polarized people and has died. When looking at church revitalization, carefully examine at what stage the church finds itself. Knowing this information can be invaluable in helping the church to re-dream its dream. He defines these stages as:

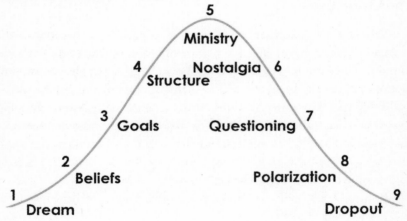

1. *The Dream Stage.* The first step in awakening a kingdom dream in a congregation is for the minister and key leaders to share a vision of the church. There are some foundational themes that provide bases for unique congregational expressions of the kingdom of God:

- A kingdom dream begins with *redemption*
- A kingdom dream envisions *God ruling*
- A kingdom dream makes Christ *concrete*
- A kingdom dream triggers *growth* and *change*

2. *The Belief Stage.* When a group of Christians pools their experiences with God in a church community, a congregational body of belief emerges. Theology becomes visible when we act out our convictions in worship, discussion, and ministry.

3. *The Goals Stage.* Church goals generally fall into two categories: mission and survival. Several strategies assist the development of dream goals:

- Keep the dream public
- Formalize goals
- Establish priorities
- State your goals specifically
- Distribute responsibility
- Evaluate at regular intervals

4. *The Structure Stage.* Everything needs some structure to work well. Organization gives the dream something to stand on and to work through.

5. *The Ministry Stage.* Ministry, from an organizational perspective, is the kingdom dream incarnated. A congregation must stay in touch with its dream, on the one hand, and its unique opportunities for ministry, on the other hand. Otherwise it may inadvertently shorten the duration of its effective ministry.

6. *The Nostalgia Stage.* After a congregation plateaus and the organizational balance tips toward degeneration, nostalgia appears. Nostalgia shows several faces:

- Nostalgia longs for a return to "the good old days"
- Nostalgia weakens our commitments to the present
- Nostalgia provides a fragile bridge to the future
- Successes, real or selected, can seduce a congregation into only looking backward
- Nostalgia's second face limits loyalty to the present
- Celebrating the past can, on occasion, provide the historical continuity for risking a confrontation with the future.

7. *The Questioning Stage.* If the concerns of nostalgic members are ignored, the organization soon moves deeper into decline. Serious questioning begins.

8. *The Polarization Stage.* If the organizational response to questioning is inadequate, the sense of doubt intensifies and polarization occurs. As polarization wedges congregational factions apart, churches may divide or at least immobilize their influences and ministries both within and beyond their membership.

9. *The Dropout Stage.* Apathy is the result of an organization remaining unresponsive to the nostalgia and differences of members.[104]

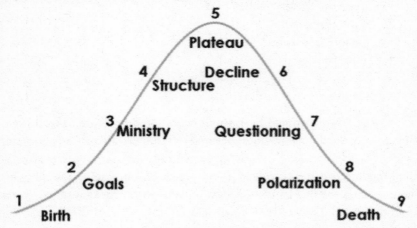

Similar bell curve based on Dale's book comes from markmillman.org.

Unfortunately, so many times when a pastor arrives at a church in need, the church has already begun the plunge down the slope of decline. The battles have already been waged and the dividing lines drawn. The people have lost their dream and are not sure that it can be recaptured.

For the established pastor, these stages may be a reality too vivid to want to revisit for the moment. As Dale's title says, the answer is for the church to dream again. Pastors must demonstrate the courage to lead the church to find their dream. The kingdom dream remains the same, but how that dream plays out in the life of the church may have changed somewhat. The community has changed, as has the congregation, the finances, and the culture. When one speaks of change, it may not necessarily just be about programming or ministry. It may be a radical step of leading the church to rediscover its purpose. Either the church finds its reason for existence or it dies.

Take time to make these evaluations. At what stage currently is the church? How quickly will the church move to the next stage? Can the church be led to dream again, either re-building on the current dream or dreaming a new dream? The church oftentimes looks to their pastor to cast vision. To initiate revitalization, become a visionary.

Dealing with Discouragement

A very real battle that pastors face at this point is discouragement. When a pastor has come under attack by members or when, upon arriving at the church deep problems of conflict are discovered, discouragement sets in. The pastor has tried to instill vision, but the clarion call to revive has been essentially ignored. What can be done at this point?

Understand That Most Everyone Gets Discouraged at Some Point. Sometimes that discouragement is a personal issue of pride. Oftentimes it is the result of unrealized dreams, rejection, or attack. If possible, find the testimonies of some of the heroes of the faith, past and present, young and old. Listen to their stories. Few in ministry have experienced nothing but success. Many have gone through the fire long before success ever arrived. Some have gone through the fire again. Some exceptions may exist but rarely does the man of God succeed without trial, and sometimes those trials cause discouragement.

Look to the Scriptures. This challenge may seem rather ridiculous to the pastor, after all, so much of the pastor's time is spent in sermon preparation and delivery. What happens, though, is that the pastor is spending time in sermon preparation and not the Word. In examining the Bible, one will find that many of the great men of faith got discouraged.

Think of Elijah for a moment. In 1 Kings 17, God uses him to raise the widow of Zarephath's son from the dead. The feat represents no small miracle in most anyone's estimation. Jump to the next chapter. Now Elijah demonstrates an incredible act of faith as he challenges the prophets of Baal to learn of the Sovereignty of the One, True God. Another miracle occurs through a demonstration of God's power through His fire, and 1 Kings 18:46 explains, "The power of the LORD was on Elijah." Finally, Elijah receives word that Queen Jezebel is determined to kill him because he had slaughtered the 450 prophets of Baal. First Kings 19:3 expounds, "Then Elijah became afraid and immediately ran for his life." The scene has turned from exaltation to desperation. The next scene finds Elijah sitting under a broom tree, wishing he would die. Here is a man who, within a matter of seemingly moments, has gone from the heights of exaltation to the pits of despair.

God, in His mercy, gives Elijah, and all men of God, the answer. The Scripture tells how God spoke to Elijah, explicating, "After the earthquake there was a fire, but the LORD was not in the fire. And after the fire there was a voice, a soft whisper. . . . Suddenly, a voice came to him and said, 'What are you doing here, Elijah?'" (1 Kings 19:12–13). When discouragement abounds in ministry, take time to listen to God. Interesting enough, Elijah was not listening. He was running. God, in His great graciousness, instead of punishing Elijah, sends him back into the battle with a message of hope (vv. 15–18). God had not forgotten Elijah, even in his frailty and fear. God does not forget the men of God today who serve Him. Sometimes it feels as though Jezebel is out to kill the pastor, and he is alone in the battle. When those feelings become overwhelming, run to God. Eventually, He will deal with the Jezebels of this world. For now, He wants the pastor to stay in the fight.

One of the mistakes that many pastors make is to get caught up in the study of God's Word for teaching and preaching and not for personal edification. I have cautioned students and pastors over the years, "Do not ever substitute sermon preparation for personal Bible study. Keep the two separate." (Go back to chapter 1 and reread the section on personal revitalization.) That information applies acutely when discouragement arises. Take time to look into the Word and see the number of God's servants who became discouraged and find hope in how God restored them.

Wait on Making Any Major Decisions. When a person gets discouraged, the overflow of negative emotion oftentimes skews good decision-making. I am certain that many pastors have resigned from churches prematurely because they were discouraged and made a rash decision based upon their feelings rather than the real facts. When discouragement occurs, set aside any major decisions until God heals the hurt. How much has the kingdom been hurt and how many times has Satan rejoiced because he was able to defeat the man of God through discouragement?

Do Not Become Isolated. When pastors get discouraged, many of them roll up into a ball and isolate themselves from everyone else. They continue to do the ministry, but they do not spend time with other pastors. Part of the problem comes from those pastors who always seem to have everything together. They are the ones who brag at the pastors' meetings of how many people they had in worship and how many baptisms took place. The discouraged pastor, on the other hand, has nothing about which to brag and thinks that he is alone. Who wants to listen to him whine anyway? Therefore, isolation sets in.

The relationships pastors build represent an essential part of ministry. This fact is important both for the discouraged pastor and for the successful leader. When a pastor gets discouraged, he needs other pastors to rally around him. When a pastor is experiencing God's blessing on his ministry, instead of rubbing that success in other's faces, he needs to look for those who are not as fortunate and be a friend to them. Paul sent Timothy to Thessalonica to strengthen those believers in their walk with Christ (1 Thess. 3:2). He also sent Tychicus to Colossae to encourage those believers and to give them an update on Paul's situation (Col. 4:7–8).[105] We all need a Paul and we all need to be a Paul.

Understanding Vision Trends

Will Mancini, the founder of Auxano, a consulting ministry that focuses on helping leaders with casting vision, offers an interesting perspective on vision-casting for the future. As quickly as culture is changing, so does vision. Understanding these trends might be helpful in laying the foundation for leading the church to find a shared vision. They also will give insight into why the church might be struggling in finding a shared vision.

- TREND #1: Expect Increasing Diversity of Opinion on What Good Vision and Strategy Look Like
- TREND #2: Articulating the Biggest Picture Will Be the Leader's Greatest Asset like Never Before
- TREND #3: The Digital World and Social Media Will Open New Possibilities for More Churches
- TREND #4: Visioning and Spiritual Formation as Disciplines Will Merge More Visibly
- TREND #5: Small Will Continue to Be the New Big
- TREND #6: Networks Are Becoming the New Denominations
- TREND #7: Leaders Will Pay More Attention to Shorter Time Horizons

- TREND #8: The Intersection of Personal and Organizational Vision Will Be Magnified
- TREND #9: Visioning Will Be Interpreted More as Making Meaning than Predicting Future
- TREND #10: External Focus and Biblical Justice Will Stay Prominent
- TREND #11: Consulting for Vision Clarity Will Surpass That for Capital Campaigns[106]

The conclusions reached by Mancini offer some important insights that demonstrate why churches and pastors struggle with vision. Vision-casting for the twenty-first-century church involves much more than just putting together a Long-Range Planning Committee and deciding how many staff, how much parking, and how much space will be needed over the next few years. This fact is especially true for churches in need of revitalization that may not even possess a vision, have an outdated vision, or are in conflict over vision. Knowing the stages churches experience in the life cycle of vision and Christians' perspectives concerning casting vision provide critical data for the revitalization pastor. Do not be discouraged by the information that is gathered. Use it to lead the church to revitalize.

Conclusion

Some important information that a pastor must glean comes from evaluating the church's vision. Sometimes a pastor arrives on a church field with a glorious vision of the future, but the church does not share that vision. Sometimes the vision of the church is skewed because the leadership has not properly ascertained potential, demographics, location, and competition. Lofty dreams are admirable, but when the pastor, pastoral staff, church leadership, and/or church members do not share in a particular vision, conflict and decline result.

Take time to evaluate the church's vision. Listen to leadership and ask specific questions. Before changes in structure, polity, or ministry become possible, the church needs to engage in a fresh casting of vision. When no vision or direction exists, the church falls into decline and the process of revitalization becomes increasingly difficult.

11

Operating through Inadequate Ministry Structures

The church in need of revitalization can often be identified as being a mimeograph organization in an iPad world. The story my staff loves the most (at least they placate me) is about the orange couch. When I arrived at a church that actually was doing very well but needed some transformation or the growth would diminish and stop, I discovered an orange couch in the pastor's office. The office itself was extremely nice. The building was new, and this couch was very much out of place. It did not match the office décor. Upon inquiry, I discovered that a couple in the church had actually found the couch out on the street to be picked up by the garbage collectors. The couple picked it up, cleaned it up as best as they could, and figured that it would look good in the pastor's office. It did not, but at the time, it was not a battle worth fighting. I finally got the finance committee to allocate money to replace it when a woman I was counseling sat on it and could not get up because the cushions were so worn. This situation did demonstrate, however, a perspective that inundated the church, an attitude that became a hindrance to the congregation's future growth.

Sometimes one might assume that revitalization is only needed for churches in decline, but even churches with a history of growth can have underlying issues that eventually will stifle the church. Inadequate or outdated structures are a primary culprit. Churches experience growth through certain methods and ministries, thinking that these ideas will carry the church into the future. Oftentimes too late, they discover that their processes do not offer adequate structure to either maintain the achieved growth or initiate continued growth in a changing world. This revelation becomes a source of conflict because people become committed to a particular ministry structure or process, missing the bigger picture of effectiveness, involvement, and impact. Therefore, the revitalization pastor has to engage the ministries and structures of the church in order to help the congregation survive and thrive.

Fellowship Structures

I do not know where I heard this stat, but a common thought is that most people get to know around fifty to sixty people in a church. While some exceptions will apply, especially for those gifted extroverts, most believers build relationships with only a select few. The dynamics of this idea changes or intensifies the longer a person is a church member. Relationships solidify over time, but they also become a hindrance to developing new relationships.

Many people like smaller churches because they offer smaller fellowship structures, but it is also why they do not really want the church to grow. In a church running one hundred people on a Sunday, they know most everyone's name and have a relationship with the vast majority of the congregation. If the congregation grows, both their level of influence and their ability to relate diminish significantly. Without direct intention, people who desire fellowship may resist growth, revitalization, and change because these things threaten the system with which they are comfortable. When the church does not provide adequate fellowship structures for growth, even if it has adequate structures for the present, the oversight becomes a hindrance.

Modern Trends

An exception to this idea arises out of twenty-first-century culture. One of the reasons that new people are not as drawn to smaller churches is because of the fact that they do not want people to know them, at least not yet. This fact is demonstrated in how people respond to being first-time guests. Many times, individuals and even families will visit a church on several occasions before they will allow anyone to know that they are visiting. Anonymity is the culture of today. In my opinion, the reason for the rise of and popularity of social media stems partly from convenience but also from privacy. A person on Facebook or Twitter can reveal what he/she wants others to know, concealing facts or details and even fabricating or deleting specifics. One can essentially become whatever a person desires through a carefully thought-out social media profile.

Therefore, larger churches offer an appeal because they allow an inconspicuousness. At the time chosen, the person or family can then seek out fellowship or make themselves known to others. People of decades ago did not follow that pattern, but churches continue to misunderstand the need for people to remain anonymous. Even today, churches embarrass newcomers by how they try to recognize them in the worship service or get information from them. Additionally, methods of personal evangelism that require "cold contacting" become incredible hindrances when people are not properly trained and when the mind-set of newcomers is not taken into consideration. I am not saying do not do door-to-door visiting. What I am saying is know the culture of the neighborhood and the people being visited. In some places it works; in others it does not.

Francis Chan, in an interview with *Outreach Magazine*, mentioned how he utilizes door-to-door visitation in working with an inner-city church. He explained,

> Everything's about context. Wherever you are, you need to figure out how to get into the lives of the unbelievers. Here, it's a little easier because they have needs, and they welcome those who want to help them. There's an immediate in. That doesn't mean that every person at every door we knock on wants to talk about Christ. That's maybe one in ten, but others, we've been able to build relationships.[107]

Thus, it is not a matter that all older systems or methods are bad or obsolete, as some might imply. To get the church growing again, know the culture in which the church is located and understand the culture of today. Utilize that information to develop fellowship systems that will help the church build relationships with its members and visitors.

The Sunday School

One of the benefits that established churches have over new church plants is a ready-made fellowship system called the Sunday school. On the negative side, some Sunday school classes are closed social systems. One way to determine this mind-set is by looking at the class roll and average attendance. Then note the number of chairs in the room. If the number of chairs equals the average attendance, most probably the class is not thinking about new people either being invited or visiting.

The ability to start new classes counterbalances any class that operates under a closed system. Starting new classes, with additional training and encouragement for teachers on the purpose of Sunday school, can also stir older classes to renew their commitment to grow and to start new classes out of their existing ones. Some classes will resist, but some will also embrace the idea.

Sunday school offers an immediate means by which to get newcomers connected to others, especially if the Sunday school provides variety in age, marital status, and gender. Since classes do not need to be large (a class of eight serves well for fellowship), most any church can bolster its fellowship systems through Bible teaching classes that meet on Sunday. Educate teachers about how the purpose of Sunday school exceeds just Bible education. The class also carries responsibilities for ministry, evangelism, discipleship, worship, and fellowship. Utilize welcome teams to connect newcomers with classes. Talk and preach about the benefits of Sunday school, even if it needs to be renamed for a more relational communication. Make sure that leadership, including pastors and deacons, are personally involved in a class.

One good way to reach newcomers and even members who do not attend Sunday school is by starting a "pastor's class." Ideally, the class meets in the sanctuary or the primary place where the church gathers for worship. The purpose of the class, in recognizing that fellowship is essential for people, is to introduce individuals to Bible study with the goal to get them into other classes that can make fellowship more accessible. Characteristics include:

- The pastor will not ask questions of the class or for any member to read or speak
- Questions are allowed from the floor if anyone is inclined to ask
- The primary method of study is lecture. Care should be taken in making sure that application is a vital part of the lecture as are assignments for applying the material for the coming week
- Allow people to sit wherever they please
- Enlist individuals or couples ahead of time who will be willing to keep roll, provide fellowship opportunities, and be aware of ministry needs
- Allow the class members to be as anonymous as they like
- Take time to meet and greet people as they enter and leave
- Use the class as an introduction to Sunday school, with the ultimate goal of moving class members to other classes

Many people respond to Sunday school in negative ways because of past experiences, perceived biases, or outright fear. Therefore, both newcomers and some longtime members never attend. Use the pastor's class to dispel these notions and to offer an entry point for Bible study, with the additional goal of getting them connected with others so that relationships are built.

Facilities

Facilities create another hindrance to fellowship. Offering opportunities for the church family to gather together outside of worship can be a challenge for churches of any size. This fact becomes especially true as the church grows. Many times churches equate food with fellowship, and while most pastors understand the theological implications of *koinōnia*, sharing in a meal is both biblical and practical. Yet, if the church facilities cannot support the entire church family in one room, this level of fellowship becomes difficult. Therefore, the pastor must develop creative ways for the church to get together.

If the church only uses the building for times of fellowship, church members possibly will develop an attitude that fellowship only occurs in the church building. Churches that offer home groups have an advantage at this point. Fellowship is far more than just meeting at a building, and it is actually bigger than just the idea of community. The book of Acts portrays the depth of community that occurred within the early church, as they met together for teaching, fellowship, communion, and prayer (Acts 2:42–46). Even as the church developed, so did the idea of fellowship. Anthony Casurella explains:

> In the later NT and other early Christian literature, fellowship is not described predominantly by the *koinōnia* ("fellowship") group of words; rather it is approached mainly through descriptions of Christians giving and receiving mutual love or through commandments that they should involve themselves by obedience. Early Christian teaching about this can be organized into three categories.
>
> 1. Fellowship and *Koinōneō*
> 2. Receiving and Giving Fellowship
> 3. Mutual Love.[108]

Evaluate the building and discover ways to create fellowship through the use of the building and beyond the facilities. Work to prevent fellowship from being solely a meal but recognize the connection that exists in these formats. Find ways in using the facilities and in being away from the building that can help the church create opportunities for community, teaching, and expressions of love.

Structure Creatively

If the worship service and/or the general church greeting provide the only means of fellowship, the church will stagnate and move into decline. As already quoted, relationships are responsible for 60 to 80 percent of people attending and joining a church. This statistic also proves to be true in keeping people. Chuck Lawless writes, "These 'people connections' are pivotal to reaching people and to keeping them. As one writer has stated, 'Newcomers don't come with Velcro already applied. It's up to the congregation to make them stick.' Relationships are a major part of the Velcro."[109] If the structures in place or the lack of structure prevents relationships from being created or developed, those structures need to be changed. In relationship building, bigger is not better. For church revitalization to occur, fellowship must be at a premium. Here are some ideas that might help the church develop relationships:

- *Be Creative with the Lord's Supper.* The early church observed an Agape Feast. Even if facilities prevent a way for the entire church to be together, share a meal on occasion followed by communion. Do the Lord's Supper in smaller groups in addition to the full congregation.

- *Use Sunday nights for fellowship.* After worship or as a part of worship, provide opportunities for the church to have time to talk together. Ice cream socials or anything similar work amazingly well, even if they seem rather old fashioned. Find ways to get people to mingle and develop relationships.

- *Go off campus.* If the facilities are a hindrance, take the church for an outing at a nearby park. Move the worship service to a place more relaxed and people friendly.

- *Encourage the church to play together.* During various holidays, have opportunities for the church to gather, invite their friends, and enjoy an evening of play. It does not have to involve a lot of expense. It is amazing how children will play without having to have inflatable rides or video games.

- *Develop Ministry Fairs and Mission Celebrations that encourage fellowship.* Many times the church does everything through a process of presentation rather than involvement. Corporate worship and presentation are critical, but fellowship becomes limited when the means become limited. Plan for how people can fellowship as they learn.

- *Be creative with baptism.* Baptisms are often limited to a worship service. Instead, take them outside, to the park, or to the river. Allow people to be directly involved through an approach that allows for fellowship to occur.

- *Take the lead in developing relationships.* Pastors are sometimes more aloof and introverted than most people realize. If the pastor is uncomfortable in group settings, relationship-building is probably going to be hindered. Pastors must determine to get out of the study and among the people. It is critical that pastors get out of their comfort zones and lead by example. Talk with people before and after the service. Be at all fellowships. Visit Sunday school classes and request invitations to parties and get-togethers. Lead by example of what fellowship should be.

- *Use a Welcome Center to greet guests.* Some facilities do not have a ready-made area for engaging people after worship. Be creative and find a way that allows the pastor to greet members and guests. If an open area is available near the worship center, develop that area for fellowship. Make it a comfortable place where people can sit and visit and where the pastor can talk with those who have attended worship. Provide coffee and make information on the church readily available.

Where fellowship is concerned, many times simple solutions are available. One just needs to evaluate the situations and be creative in providing ways for fellowship to occur.

Ministry Structures

How does the church minister to its members? When a church is smaller, the pastor, both by design and by expectation, handles most of the ministry in the church. This fact alone demonstrates why many small churches cannot get over certain attendance barriers. One person can only meet the needs of so many people, then the ministry begins to fail.

The Ministry of the Early Church

The early church faced the problem of meeting ministry needs. The church had experienced incredible, immediate growth at its birth. Three thousand people came to Christ at Pentecost, and through the preaching of the gospel and the witness of the church, "every day the Lord added to them those who were being saved" (Acts 2:47). Ministry was being provided, and the church involved itself corporately in meeting needs as "those who believed were of one heart and mind, and no one said that any of his possessions was his own, but instead they held everything in common" (Acts 4:32). Yet, problems arose and the ministry began to suffer, even under the administration of the apostles. Thus, the prototype for deacon service arose in Acts 6 with the appointment of the seven to oversee the ministry to the widows.

At this point, the ministry structure of the church began to change. Even the first-century church in its infancy experienced growing pains. Growth causes problems. Understand that fact. When structures are not adapted for meeting these challenges, then the church begins to stagnate and decline. The early church met the ministry needs and "the preaching about God flourished, the number of the disciples in Jerusalem multiplied greatly, and a large number of priests became obedient to the faith" (Acts 6:7). Fixing ministry problems increases evangelistic outreach. The church's integrity remained intact, and the church began to reach the unreachable.

Think about this miracle. The party of the high priest and his associates was identified with the Sadducees (Acts 4:1; 5:17), a religious sect in Jesus' day who desired to maintain the priestly caste and who held the majority of seats in the ruling body called the Sanhedrin.[110] They offered the sacrifices and took care of the temple but rejected the very theological foundation of their service. They denied miracles, the resurrection (Mark 12:27), and rejected the oral tradition of the Pharisees. Yet through the change in ministry structure that allowed for greater growth and service, even these who would be very hard to reach came to Christ. That in itself shows what happens when the church expands and revitalizes its ministry structures.

Change

If the church is going to grow, meeting people's needs must become a ministry that is shared and is broken down into small units. With widow care, hospitals, counseling, senior adults, and a vast number of other needs that go on within the context of the church family, it is easy to understand how ministry gets bogged down and becomes a hindering factor in church revitalization. The fact that church members resist changing the current ministry structure only exasperates the problem. They like having the pastor being available for hospital visitation, home ministry, and counseling. These issues create a huge dilemma for the church. To grow, it must change its structures, but a change in structure means that the delivery method of ministry changes. Therefore, an impasse occurs, conflict arises, and the church falls deeper into a need for revitalization.

So what process should a pastor follow in order to bring about a change in ministry structures that will allow for an expansion in numbers but also in the ministry implementation?

Biblically Educate Members. Before undertaking any changes, lead the church through Bible study and preaching that helps them understand pastoral roles, leadership roles, the work of the church, and the responsibility of membership (see chapter 14). Oftentimes, members base their expectations from an entitlement mentality, and therefore they maintain an unhealthy understanding of ministry and ministry partnership. Other times, past experiences, or history dictates their expectations. Therefore, a new understanding must be communicated. This process takes time, so do not initiate any structure changes without investing the efforts to get the message understood.

Change Expectations. Work within the current structures to change the expectations of those ministries. Members struggle to serve because, in many churches, the various committees and classes do nothing in actual service. They function because the church has always had that particular committee or has always offered that particular program but with no real purpose. Examine the current structure and see what can be utilized to increase ministry effectiveness. Change does not always have to be extreme. It can be effective in just adjustment and involvement.

Use the Sunday School. The Sunday school not only provides an immediate solution to fellowship problems but also ministry issues. Not every class will get on board but meet with those teachers and leaders who demonstrate a desire to serve their members. If time has properly been invested in biblical teaching, the Holy Spirit will stir up those who have a heart to serve. Start with those classes and release them to serve. Allow them to educate their members on ministry needs. Through the Sunday school, teachers and members can discover needs within the class, meet those needs, and communicate with the pastor when further ministry is necessary.

Give the Ministry Away. The pastor may be at fault as to why the ministry has never expanded. Some pastors struggle with delegation, not to mention meeting the expectation of members. Fear of conflict and the ego all play into the way in which ministry gets done. The pastor not only must teach the congregation about biblical ministry structures, but he must also be willing to study and apply biblical principles himself. In order to grow the ministry, the ministry must be shared with others.

Mentor Potential Ministers. One of the reasons that people do not minister to others is because they do not know how. In the mind of the pastor, the work of the ministry is easy. Many laypeople, however, in taking the ministry as seriously as they do, are afraid to step out and serve because they might make a mistake that affects the spiritual growth or vitality of another person. This same reason impacts evangelism. Untrained believers often do not witness, not because they do not believe in the lostness of humanity, but because they understand the severity of making a mistake. Therefore, the easiest way to handle ministry and evangelism is not do them. The pastor can overcome this simple problem by educating and mentoring those who demonstrate an interest in ministry. Take them to the hospital, talk with them about the possible obstacles or questions they may face in ministry, let them be observant of a pastor in action, then send them out to minister. Jesus sending out the seventy offers a picture of this process. They observed how He witnessed and ministered. He mentored them, then sent them out (read the earlier chapters, then read Luke 10:1–12).

Use the Deacon Body.[111] In so many cases, a primary reason for church decline stems from conflict within the church, specifically between the deacons and the pastor. At times, both parties share the guilt of sinful power struggles. They attempt to use biblical force to justify their positions, but sin and ego lay at the root of the source. The pastor must take time to mentor the deacons concerning their vital role in the church. In many new church plants, a deacon body is not even considered because of these struggles. The established church does not have such a luxury. Although Wake Forest University calls itself the Demon Deacons, not all deacons are demons. Many times conflict occurs because of a lack of discipleship, poor examples in deacon leadership, and boredom. If the deacons only meet to talk about problems, then problems will arise. Therefore, get the deacons on the ministry field:

- Mentor those who are interested
- Release those who are ready

- Use those who serve well and brag on them
- Trust the process to work
- Review the biblical qualifications of deacons in 1 Timothy 3:8–13 with the deacon officers and deacon body
- Request time in meetings to disciple the deacons on their responsibilities
- Model for them the biblical requirements for a pastor
- Develop with the deacons a covenant of service and ministry[112]
- Build relationships with the deacons

Shared ministry is not about denying the pastor's biblical role or leadership. It is not about shunning responsibility. It entails finding better ways to break ministry down into smaller parts and units so that more ministry can take place. A key understanding at which all Christians must arrive is that *when ministry occurs, all of it is done in the name of Jesus, regardless of whether it is the pastor or another believer being used to offer the ministry.*

Leadership/Governance Structures

Every church has to have some form of governance or polity. Without leadership structure, decisions will not be made, ministry will suffer, and the church will fail. Leadership, however, is one of those innocuous concepts that people try to define but honestly cannot. Scores of books have been written on leadership, yet definitions vary by peculiarities of personality, character traits, goal-setting, and achievement. I have already addressed the issue of agreeing with MacArthur regarding the issue that, for pastors, the call is not to be just leaders but servant-leaders. John Piper concurs, "At a men's retreat I defined *spiritual leadership* as 'knowing where God wants people to be and taking the initiative to get them there by *God's* means in reliance on *God's* power.' I suggested that the way we find out where God wants people to be is to ask where God Himself is going . . . that He aims to magnify His glory in all He does."[113] The writings of Jonathan Edwards, a leader of the First Great Awakening from the eighteenth century, denote this same perspective:

God and the creature, in the emanation of the divine fulness, are not properly set in opposition; or made the opposite parts of a disjunction. Nor ought God's glory and the creature's good, to be viewed as if they were properly and entirely distinct, in the objection. . . . God in seeking his glory, seeks the good of his creatures; because the emanation of his glory (which he seeks and delights in, as he delights in himself and his own eternal glory) implies the communicated excellency and happiness of his creatures. And in communicating his fulness for them, he does it for himself; because their good, which he seeks, is so much in union and communion with himself. God is their good. Their excellency and happiness is nothing, but the emanation and expression of God's glory: God, in seeking their glory and happiness, seeks himself: and in seeking himself, *i.e.,* himself diffused and expressed, (which he delights in, as he delights in his own beauty and fulness) he seeks their glory and happiness.[114]

Notice what Edwards suggests. It is not that Christians are not leaders (though he does not use that term). Believers, however, should not seek their own excellency or glory, but they should seek to glorify God in all that they do. That perspective defines biblical leadership.

Church Governance Reviewed

The church does not always function the way that Piper and Edwards suggest. Sin nature mars biblical ideal. Every church faces that fact, and it becomes most evident in how churches govern themselves. Leadership, in the midst of these governing structures, becomes a critical feature. In a recent survey, the top five reasons for pastoral termination were:

1. Control issues—who is going to run the church
2. Poor people skills on the part of the pastor
3. Pastor's leadership style—too strong
4. Church was already conflicted when pastor arrived
5. Pastor's leadership style—too weak[115]

Notice the obvious paradox and perhaps hypocrisy. Churches terminate pastors because their leadership style is too strong or too weak. No wonder church revitalization is so desperately needed. Church members, and even pastors, have made the church all about themselves and very little about God, resulting in conflict, termination, and decline.

What many pastors do not recognize in accepting an established church, especially ones that date back at least a century, is the history of leadership in the church. Today, church planting is being led by pastors and pastoral staff, sometimes sent out intentionally by another church or denominational missions organization, and other times through their own initiative to plant a church in a particular city or region. Many of those churches begin with a governance structure that allows the pastor to be seen as the clear leader. Elder-led models have become quite popular in response to the power struggles experienced in many established churches.

These established churches, however, did not have their beginnings like many church starts today. They began through the desire of a local group of laypeople, wanting to start a church in a particular part of town. Every church I have pastored had this type of beginning. Sometimes pastoral leadership would be involved in the launch. Other times, years would pass before they would hire a pastor. Many of these churches struggled in the beginning years. Laypeople sacrificed in order to have a church. My grandfather, for example, mortgaged his home in order to start a church in Knoxville, Tennessee, with six other men nearly a century ago. During times of financial distress, anxious uncertainty, internal crises, and external hindrances, the laypeople were the ones who stuck by the church, supported the church, and kept the church afloat. They have watched pastors come and go, declaring, "the Lord has led them to a new place of service." All the while, many of these pastors left the church "high and dry," and the laypeople knew it. Now enter the new pastor with lofty dreams and high ideals. Go back to chapter 2 on stakeholders in the church, and once again these conflicts and uncertainties become more understandable. Church governance fell onto the shoulders of laypeople, not pastors.

Add to that dilemma the training many laypeople received in how the church should operate. In many scenarios, the administration of the local corporation reflected more on the church than did the Bible. Church polity directed that the pastor serve as chairman and the deacons as the board of directors of the church. Church governance in states that require a Board of Trustees in order for the church to incorporate emulates this same directive, resulting in confused roles and sometimes conflict.

Pastors of established churches need to understand that this conflict and debate surrounding authority and leadership are nothing new. Robert Naylor, in his book published in 1955 entitled *The Baptist Deacon,* asks a question regarding the necessity of deacons in the church. In seeking an answer, he writes, "There is another occasion for the question of need being raised. Tension between pastor and deacons is no uncommon experience in churches. Often this has come to open warfare, and the resulting tragedy has crippled the influence and work of such churches."[116] Richard Niebuhr also understands this tension as he opines with regard to the loss of pastoral authority: "But the loss of this authority seems due far more to the rise of a large and varied group of learned men in many other professions than to a failure on the part of the Church and ministry as such to maintain previously established standards."[117] Even Jonathan Edwards, with all of his notoriety and published works, was fired from his Northampton pulpit, only to land in Stockbridge, Massachusetts, to work as a pastor and missionary to the Housatonic Indians. There he found that relatives of some of those who demanded his resignation in Northampton attended this new church and worked in the school at Stockbridge. This tension eventually escalated to the point that Edwards left to assume the presidency of the College of New Jersey. Governance and polity problems have always plagued the church. The church today is no different from the church of the 1950s or the 1750s.

Evaluation

Just as the pastor must make evaluations regarding fellowship and ministry, it is important for the pastor to understand the present leadership model in place, how that model will affect the future direction of the church, and how he will be able to work within that structure or make changes. While debate will always surround which system works best or is most biblical, what the pastor really needs to determine is effectiveness. Obviously, unbiblical systems will stifle the Holy Spirit's work within the church, but God is still bigger than any system. Sometimes revitalization is necessary and becomes evident because the leadership structures hinder the church. These problems demonstrate why longer-term pastorates are necessary for revitalization. Most probably, a pastor is not going to change leadership structures within a couple of years, or at least live to tell about it!

Unchanging Structures. Some churches, because of their denominational affiliations or oversight, cannot change leadership structures. In these cases, the pastor must distinctively look at how he can work within those structures. The key issue at this point is to make sure that the structure in place helps the church move to the next level. The pastor needs to ask these questions:

- What structure is currently in place?
- What improvements could be made to this structure?
- What hindrances are present that will prevent revitalization and growth?
- Will the church/denomination be open to allowing any changes in leadership structure?
- What hindrances to church revitalization are present because of the current leadership structures?
- Are there any ways to work within the system, while at the same time, prevent the hindrances from affecting the church?

Changing Structures. Other churches are built upon a polity that allows for change and re-tooling of some leadership structures. In my opinion, changing the leadership structures probably is the most difficult task in the established church. While the constitution and by-laws may permit changes that move decision-making and leadership to new groups or individuals, this action can lead to responses that vary from hurt feelings to real anger to church splits. The fear of these responses should not prevent the pastor from making these changes. He must be aware, though, that when charges about poor leadership surface, they often occur in response to this type of change. In order to accomplish this task, note these ideas:

- Go slow
- Demonstrate great care in making changes
- Communicate well with the church
- Bathe the process in intense prayer
- Go slow

- Have proper information available
- Think ahead of time of questions and answers
- Go slow

Organizational Structures

Churches operate under an assortment of organization styles and a number of variations within those structures. Depending on the author or speaker, one can find proponents for every type of style presently utilized in the church setting. The key issue is not the style itself. The real question surrounds whether or not that particular structure can lead the church through revitalization and into growth. The pastor and leadership have to answer that question. It is not about parroting what another growing church does. The church in need of revitalization must determine what system and variants within that system will get the church out of its decline and into stability and growth. Some important thoughts to remember:

- If power corrupts, absolute power corrupts absolutely. Sometimes the pastor thinks that the solution to the leadership problem is for the pastor to make all of the decisions. I am a strong proponent of pastoral leadership. Read Hebrews 13:7–17 and Ephesians 4:11–12 for a couple of biblical examples. The problem, however, is that pastors need some form of accountability as do laypeople. A power group of pastors is no different than a power group of laypeople. Sin is sin.
- Members must be included and must accept an active role in implementing a strategy change. A change in their attitude probably will need to precede any change in structure.
- Every church is different. A cookie-cutter leadership style or process may spell doom for a particular congregation that may not have a pastor who can handle the level of responsibility that others can oversee.
- Pastors must be willing, if they are going to lead into growth, to move from being a shepherd (I take care of everyone) to being a rancher (I take care of the caretakers who take care of everyone).

The pastor must constantly be aware of and deal with the factors
in the church organization that keep it from growing.

- Pastors must guard against a small church, dying church mentality and prevent these ideas from creeping back into the church.

Conclusion

Church revitalization demands much more than just a desire to grow.
One must be willing to take the risk of evaluating structures within the
church that prevent the congregation from moving away from its pattern
of decline and to discover ways to grow again. This process of evaluation
is ongoing. Particular changes in ministry, fellowship, and leadership
may help the church achieve certain goals, but those same changes, when
they are not tweaked and reevaluated, can actually become hindrances
to the church moving to the next level. Churches that refuse to change
their structure will struggle to revitalize. Therefore, carefully evaluate the
structures of the church. Find which ones are the easiest to change and
make those adjustments. Those successes can then lead to other changes.
Evaluate which structures will be the most difficult and the most resisted
and proceed cautiously as those turbulent waters are navigated. Do not
change something just for the sake of change. Change it because the
structure in place hinders the work of revitalization.

CHAPTER

12

Failure to Increase the Impact of Ministry

Most churches do some form of ministry. Many churches that are in need of revitalization end up performing ministry more for themselves than they do for the community. This oversight results in a great hindrance to revitalization because it overlooks the very people who are in need and are prospects. This issue is one of the most critical for the declining church. The natural response to decline is self-preservation, a reaction that is deadly and must be overcome.

The revitalization pastor must lead the church to look beyond itself once again. History most probably reveals that, at one time, the church ministered to and reached the unchurched. For a number of reasons, the church slowly moved away from looking outward and began to focus on itself. The more it looked inward, the more it declined. The pastor must lead the church to reverse those trends and to move once again toward ministry and outreach.

Expectations

The church today faces a great deal of competition in trying to reach people. In the days of old, most everything revolved around the church

189

building. People went to church, not just to worship, but to fellowship, meet people, and enjoy activities. Fast-forward a few decades and now church buildings sit idle while malls, pizza playgrounds, and ball parks are all filled to capacity. With cable TV, video games, and twenty-four-hour Walmarts, people can find something to do at any time they wish, day and night. Churches have lost their impact, their voice, and thus their outreach. In order to regain a hearing from the world, the church must get back to doing ministry that meets the needs of people outside of the church.

Servant Evangelism

One process that accentuates the church's mission and ministry is servant evangelism. The combination of these two concepts lead the church to be able to accomplish ministering to its own body, serving those outside of the congregation, and evangelizing those who do not know Christ. The beauty of this ministry is that it helps the church keep a proper balance between evangelism and ministry. Just like evangelism and discipleship, evangelism and ministry are not mutually excluding ideas. They actually work well together. The classic example is Jesus and the woman at the well. In the kindness that Jesus showed this woman, it led to her believing and to the belief of others in Sychar. Ultimately, Paul reminded the Philippian Christians to have this mind of Christ, whereby "He emptied Himself by assuming the form of a slave" (Phil. 2:7). Throughout Jesus' ministry, as He loved on people, doors opened for Him to preach and teach. That process is called servant evangelism. Through servant evangelism, Christians intentionally meet people's needs and model service in order to share the gospel more effectively. In a world that denies biblical truth and the importance of the church, this method of outreach serves well to help the church regain its voice and to demonstrate that the church cares beyond itself.

The Servant Evangelism Blitz

How does the church go about starting a servant evangelism ministry? Obviously, as with most new ministries, it needs to start out small. Preach on service and ministering to the community, then lead the church to conduct a one-day Servant Evangelism Blitz. One of the great benefits of this ministry is that it will appeal to more believers than does a model presentation type of evangelism. As already noted, people always need to be trained in how to share their faith. The fact is, though, some people are not spiritually ready for initiative evangelism. That fact is the reality of the church. If the only means of evangelism offered is through learning a model presentation, many church members will never get involved.

Servant evangelism bridges this gap. Those who are afraid of initiative evangelism will see that this form of outreach removes those perceived barriers. Thus, a larger number of people will be involved. Once they see how God can use them through this method, training them in other methods will become easier. Servant evangelism is not the sole answer to church revitalization and evangelism. It is one way, though, to get the church thinking beyond itself.

Some suggestions for making this day successful are:

1. Establish places of service ahead of time. Avoid doing work, such as lawn care or fence painting, that does not allow people to engage others in some form of conversation. Sometimes in the beginning, just doing some form of service opens opportunities to cause people to take note of the church. These types of projects are beneficial especially for getting church members involved who have never reached out to anyone before. The projects, however, will eventually lose appeal and impact because the community may never know that this work was done, thus the church's influence has not changed.

2. Have shirts printed that identify those involved in this ministry, using especially the name of the church and/or a Bible reference to service. Do not print them with Servant Evangelism Blitz. (I made that mistake.)

3. Train your people that servant evangelism is the in-house name for this outreach. Within the community, talk about doing service projects.

4. Have a specific time for the projects to begin and end on a particular day. Offer a variety of opportunities and even times for the projects to take place. If they can all start on a Saturday morning, it is very beneficial to have everyone meet at the church to pray together before setting out for a day of service. That one act will build fellowship, support, and excitement.

5. Celebrate the victories with the church. Allow people to share testimonies, have video or still pictures, and thank and recognize those who participated. If any specific results occurred, communicate them with the congregation.

6. Do not fret about getting information on people to whom the church ministers if the church meets them away from their homes. Make sure that teams have plenty of information that they can give away on the church. When asked why they are doing these projects, simply respond that the church is out serving the community so that they will know that the church cares about them.

7. Have the eventual goal to make servant evangelism an ongoing ministry in the church, specifically using the Sunday school as the primary vehicle.

Ongoing Servant Evangelism

Once the church catches the fire of servant evangelism and begins to see the benefit of this type of ministry, many of those involved will want the opportunity to do servant evangelism throughout the year. At this point, the church has reached an important milestone because it is beginning to look beyond internal ministry and is rebuilding a reputation in the community. The following is a suggested process for enrolling, engaging, and equipping Sunday school classes to do servant evangelism as ongoing projects within the community.

CALVARY ♥ . . .

Beginning January 26 during the Great Commission Mobilization Day, we are encouraging all Life Groups and/or individuals to commit and participate in Calvary Loves . . .

What is the purpose of Calvary Loves . . . ?

Our purpose is to mobilize our church body to get outside the church to meet new people, develop new relationships with individuals, be salt and light in the community, and create opportunities to minister to people, families, schools, etc., in our community.

What is the goal of Calvary Loves . . . ?

Our goal is to get more people within our church involved and engaged in ministry within the community, being salt and light for Christ. These ministry projects will give us opportunities to invite people to church, engage in spiritual discussions, share the story of Jesus Christ and His love for the world, and show people that Calvary Loves . . .

What is the challenge for individuals and Life Groups within Calvary?

1. Select the county in which your class would like to serve on an on-going basis (3–4 times a year or more) in Fayette, Jessamine, or Scott counties.

2. Determine what your ministry will be: a public school, neighborhood, community organization, athletic team, etc. Discuss possible built-in relationships, connections, and/or opportunities someone may already have within your Life Group where you as a group can serve.

- *Do you have any school faculty (teacher, principal, etc.) within your Life Group?*
- *Do you know any athletic coaches?*
- *Do you know any business owners or local business employees to whom you could minister?*

- *Do you have any Public Safety personnel (i.e., Police, Firemen, etc.) in your Life Group?*
- *Do you know of any on-going needs in the community that are not being met by any other church, ministry organization, etc.?*

3. Determine the types of projects your class could do on an on-going basis (serving food, tutoring students, working concessions for a local high school along with boosters, etc.) throughout the year.

Suggested ideas for serving

1. Establish contact with a public school (Principal, Resource Counselor, Teacher) and see what needs exist that your class could meet, such as tutoring students, helping with "Open House" nights serving food/drinks, providing breakfast or lunch for a school faculty and sharing word of encouragement to them, etc.

2. Look for opportunities in the community that could be useful and beneficial. (Ex: Delivering care packages and praying for patients/family members in hospitals, sponsoring a local sports team and providing snacks, or covering a concession stand.

3. Adopt one of the Lexington Police Dept. Roll Calls (three shifts working each day) or a Lexington Firehouse.

4. The sky is the limit with multiple opportunities. Be prayerfully creative and seek where God is leading you.

Project Requirements

1. All projects must be done with the spirit and intention of personal evangelism. We ask that these projects be carried out with the desire to interact and develop new relationships, to share the gospel with individuals and groups when the opportunity presents itself, and to look for opportunities to invite people to PMBC for worship and spiritual growth.

2. All projects must be carried out in the spirit of doing something beneficial and useful for multiple people (school, business, etc.), not just a single person or family. We do encourage your class to minister to individuals and families when a need arises throughout the year, but this will not be considered a "Calvary Loves . . ." Project. Projects are to be in the same spirit as our recent Servant Evangelism Blitz projects. *Note: Picking up litter along the road or painting a fence in someone's backyard, etc., are not desired projects.*

3. All Life Groups and/or individuals are encouraged to serve in 3–4 projects (or more) throughout the year. Discover what needs exist and determine when these needs can be addressed by coordinating with ministry target. By offering assistance or ministry several times throughout the year, we get a chance to meet and develop relationships with people we otherwise would never meet. These projects broaden our "circles of influence" in the community and give us opportunities to share Christ.

4. All projects must be coordinated, carried out, and largely funded by the Life Group and/or individuals. It is up to your class to carry out and fulfill these projects. Classes are encouraged to invest their time, talent, and treasure into these projects. Some financial assistance can be given through the Community Outreach budget on a case-by-case basis. Ultimate approval will come through the Pastor of Missions & Evangelism when submitted.

5. Projects need to be created where no other church, ministry, and/or organization currently exists. This clarification means organizations such as the Salvation Army, Ronald McDonald House, etc., would not be considered viable ministry options since they are already being funded and supported by a host of other agencies, churches, etc.

6. All projects must be presented and approved by the Pastor of Missions & Evangelism prior to scheduling and fulfilling to ensure ministry consistency and effectiveness in the community.

Life Group Organization/Leadership

1. Each Life Group is encouraged to select at least two individuals to be "Calvary Loves . . ." Life Group coordinators to:

- *Establish contact with potential ministry area*
- *Organize and coordinate outreach event*

- *Communicate information to Life Group*
- *Collect money from within Life Group to fund projects*
- *Purchase materials and items necessary for event.*

*Life Group Teachers/Leaders are encouraged to give this responsibility to others within the class.

2. Each Life Group is asked to fund and financially support as much of these projects as possible. If church assistance is needed, it must be requested and approved by the Pastor of Missions & Evangelism prior to purchasing materials and scheduling in a reasonable amount of time prior to the event.

3. Determine the number of projects your class will coordinate and fulfill. Three to four projects for the year are suggested.

4. If projects are larger and more time demanding, your class can partner with another Life Group.

5. All projects must be documented and report upon completion to the Pastor of Missions & Evangelism.

6. Projects must not interrupt or conflict with ministry target goals.

> **Example:** Do not have a cookout and giveaway "free" food and drinks in front of a high school football stadium, thus undercutting the booster club concession sales. Do not give away free food/drinks in front of businesses that sell food/drinks. Think through how your ministry project would affect not only your ministry target but surrounding businesses, people, and/or organizations you are trying to engage.

Project Submittal Deadline:

Sunday January 26 from 5–7:30 p.m. both Life Groups and individuals will have the opportunity to sign up or volunteer to be involved in this ministry emphasis at the Calvary Loves . . . table.

Conclusion

When the church no longer ministers to its community, it loses its privilege to speak. Couple that fact with any number of other variables that hinder the church's reputation and one can easily understand why many churches have fallen into decline. Revitalization becomes necessary, not only for the church that exhibits all the signs of being plateaued, but also for the church that appears to be solid externally. Things may be well today, but the church will eventually begin its downslide if it becomes internalized.

Expanding the church's ministry allows the church to turn around this decline. It serves as a visible sign that the congregation has not given up. Life still goes on, and the church will survive. Examine the ministries and lead the church to serve.

13

The Church Lacks Important Ingredients for Conversion Growth

f the church is not reaching people, the church will not grow. One might consider biological growth (the conversion of church members' children) as a sustainable strategy, but it is not. Therefore, the church must provide the important ingredients to make conversion growth possible. This idea, in no way, presumes upon the sovereignty of God in salvation, but we must also recognize that God uses means to bring people to Christ. In order for the church to grow and to revitalize, it must effectively provide and perfect these means.

An Effective Prayer Ministry

When all else fails, read the instructions; when all else fails, pray. Unfortunately, many churches follow this pattern. Prayer becomes the last resort, not the first. If the need for revitalization does anything, it should drive the church to its knees. Before it can revitalize, the church must connect with God. Jim Nicodem offers some excellent suggestions on how to get the church praying:

1. Set a Good Example. Pray as the leader and share stories of its benefit.
2. Pray as a Staff.
3. Teach Regularly on the Topic of Prayer.
4. Include Prayer Exercises in the Worship Services. Be creative during the pastoral prayer time and include others in praying in the service. Nicodem suggests praying the Armor of God of Ephesians 6 as an example.
5. Weave Prayer Throughout Leadership Meetings. Do not just begin or end the meeting in prayer. When a need arises or a concern, take time that very moment to pray.
6. Train Small Group Leaders to Protect Time for Prayer.
7. Provide Prayer Counselors at the End of Worship Services.[118]

Unfortunately, many churches do not have a strong prayer ministry. It is, from an honest perspective, a very difficult ministry to keep going. Most pastors can mobilize their churches to pray over a specific task or during a short season. A consistent prayer ministry that involves groups of people praying weekly offers a much greater challenge. For revitalization to happen, prayer must be at the forefront. Ron Jenson and Jim Stephens concur: "If we are to see quantitative, qualitative, and organic growth of the church, we must take prayer much more seriously than we have in the past. . . . The lack of a sense of needing God diminishes our sense of need to pray. Anemic corporate prayer reflects our lack of understanding about the supernatural processes at work in church growth."[119]

The following are suggestions for how prayer can be incorporated into a variety of ministries and activities in the church. All that the church does should be bathed in prayer.

Develop a Mission Statement

- To encourage and equip the church family by demonstrating our love for one another through an effective Prayer Ministry.
- To prayerfully support the church's effort to lead people to faith in Christ.
- To intercede for the spiritual and physical needs of our church family, community, and others.

- To record prayers and petitions before God, so that when His answers come, the church can bear witness of His activity.

Offer Prayer Ministry Opportunities

- *Intercessory Prayer Ministry:* Requests are submitted and placed in a notebook in the intercessory prayer room and members who have signed up commit themselves to pray in the room for one hour per week on a specific day and time for those requests. Requests are submitted through:
  1. Emergency cell phone
  2. Church website
  3. Prayerline checked every morning and evening
- *Emergency Prayer Chain:* Requests submitted through emergency cell phone or through the church office
- *Youth Prayer Support*
  1. Monthly prayer calendar is placed in magazine racks by Welcome Center to encourage members to pray for students and leaders.
  2. Parents meet to pray on Mondays in the worship center with the Monday night prayer ministry. Prayer walk for a different school the last Saturday of the month.
- *Ministry Support:* This idea entails "enlisting" people to pray for special events such as: National Day of Prayer, Large Evangelistic Events, Men's Night Out, Women's special events, VBS teachers and workers, Upward Basketball workers and coaches, Student trips.
- *Sending Out Support:* This ministry is also an "enlisting" job, but mostly for mission trips that happen starting in the spring and running usually through early fall.
- *Monday Prayer Ministry:* Small groups meet every Monday night at 6:30 p.m. to pray for guests from the preceding Sunday and for those who will be contacting them as opportunities arise. The groups also pray for other church matters such as revival, special events, the nation, missionaries, etc. Anyone can come and pray during the semester on any Monday night.

- *Wednesday Night "Kingdom Praying":* This ministry is a ten- to fifteen-minute guided prayer time before the preaching of the Word that helps the church focus on "Kingdom" issues of the church or nation. It is normally led by a staff member but can change at any time.
- *Weekly Prayer Bulletin:* This publication is made available every Wednesday night and is e-mailed to all prayer group leaders. It encourages the church body to pray at home during the week.
- *Bulletin Board:* The bulletin board is located in a heavily traveled area, is used as a reminder to pray, and is updated periodically.
- *New Member/ Discover Class:* Someone from the prayer team is asked to come and talk about the prayer opportunities within the church. We coach them on how to get involved.

Develop Weekly Prayer Teams / 100 Prayer Partner Teams

Prayer Group Leader Job Description:

Being a Prayer Group Leader is an exciting adventure and a wonderful way to build meaningful relationships. Throughout God's Word, we are instructed to pray for ourselves and for others. Intercession is a tremendous privilege and an area in which we often see life-changing results. The 100 Prayer Partner Teams are encouraged to be committed to a weekly time of "getting in touch with the heart of God" on behalf of the ministries and staff of the church.

Listed below are the requirements for being a Prayer Group Leader in the 100 Prayer Partner Teams. As a Prayer Group Leader, I am committed to:

1. Keeping myself clean and pure in my walk with the Lord by being thoroughly honest in my confession of sin on a daily basis.
2. Being accountable to my group for a regular time of prayer once a week, starting and ending on time.
3. Establishing guidelines that everyone understands in order to avoid confusion and misunderstanding.
4. Seeking actively to add new members to my 100 Prayer Partner Team.

5. Encouraging my group to be accountable to each other in areas of attendance, faithfulness, and godliness in our personal lives.
6. Committing the majority of one hour together in prayer for the church and staff in the areas listed in the Weekly Prayer Bulletin.
7. Defending the church and staff against the powers of darkness that would try to undermine the power of God in our midst.
8. Being creative in my prayer walk to avoid complacency in my group.
9. Building up the body of Christ by avoiding any gossip or unkind remarks.
10. Notifying the Prayer Ministry Coordinator of changes in my group, i.e., adding members, change of time or place.

Prayer Ministry Mission Statement:

- To encourage and equip the church family by demonstrating our love for one another through an effective Prayer Ministry
- To prayerfully support the church's efforts to lead people to faith in Christ
- To intercede for the spiritual and physical needs of our church family, community, and others
- To record prayers and petitions before God, so that when His answers come, the church can bear witness of His activity

Since the neglect of prayer serves as a primary dysfunction and hindrance to the church, lead the church to pray. Make corporate, personal, and group prayer a primary focus and stay on task to keep prayer at the center of the church's work.

A Good Percentage of Weekly Guests

If the church does not see new people attending worship or other ministries, the church will not grow. There is nothing new about that idea. Earlier chapters have already visited the hindrances to growth and reaching new people. Rick Ezell's article on first-time guests offers some helpful reminders at this point. Ezell writes, "Healthy and growing churches pay close attention to the people they count as members, as well as those people who are not yet a part of the flock. These people know that new people are the lifeblood of a growing church."[120] These five ideas include:

1. **Visitors make up their minds regarding a new church in the first ten minutes of their visit.** What that idea means is that churches need to spend as much time in preparing for and greeting guests as they do in preparing for the worship service. Some questions to ask include:

- Are parking attendants in place?
- Is there appropriate signage?
- Are your ushers and greeters performing the "right" job?
- Is the environment you take for granted user-friendly and accepting to guests?

2. **Most church members are not friendly.** Consider these ideas:

- Observe to see if your members greet guests with the same intensity and concern before and after the worship service as they do during a formal time of greeting in the worship service.
- The six most important minutes of a church service, in a visitor's eyes, are the three minutes before the service and the three minutes after the service. A church would be wise to discover its most gregarious and welcoming members and deploy them as unofficial greeters before and after each service, in addition to being the designated parking-lot greeters, door greeters, ushers, and informational booth personnel.
- Do not make promises the church cannot keep.

3. **Church guests are highly consumer-oriented.** Some ways to work through this obstacle include:

- Look at the church through the eyes of a first-time guest.
- Use some objective, yet trained, anonymous guests to give an honest appraisal of the church and the worship service.

4. **The church is in the hospitality business.** Because kingdom business far outweighs secular business, the church should not seek to offer anything less.

- *Hospitality* is almost a forgotten word and needs revitalization.

- Church members can extend hospitality by sitting with guests during the service, by giving a tour of the facilities, by inviting them to lunch after the service, or by connecting with them later in the week.

5. **You only have one chance to make a good impression.** Consider these questions:

- Are you creating a good experience, beginning with your parking lot?
- Are you consciously working to remove barriers that make it difficult for guests to find their way around and to feel at home with your people?
- Do newcomers have all the information they need without having to ask any embarrassing questions?
- Are your greeters and ushers on the job, attending to details and anticipating needs before they are expressed?
- Does anything about your guests' first experience make them say, "Wow!" and want to return?[121]

Evaluate how effectively the church is in attracting and keeping new people. Lead the church to correct those things that hinder new growth and help them develop a passion for reaching new people. When church members begin inviting new people to attend and those guests return, church revitalization is taking place.

A Commitment to Evangelism and Discipleship

Most Christians talk about reaching others, but it rarely becomes a genuine passion and burden in their lives. Few people witness and fewer people see their witness bear fruit. In order to revitalize, the church has to rediscover its passion for Great Commission evangelism. Thom Rainer offers ten questions that a pastor can ask to help analyze the church's passion for evangelism. These questions are also insightful because they can demonstrate how far away or how close a church is to revitalization and the obstacles it must overcome. Rainer asks:

1. Are members more concerned about the lost than their own preferences and comfort? Listen to how church members talk to understand what their true priorities are.
2. Is the church led to pray for lost persons? Most churches are pretty good about praying for those who have physical needs. But do they pray for those who have the greatest spiritual need, a relationship with Jesus Christ?
3. Are the members of the church open to reaching people who don't look or act like them? The gospel breaks all racial, ethnic, and language barriers. Do the members seek to reach others? Do they rejoice when these people become a part of the church?
4. Do conflicts and critics zap the evangelistic energy of the church? An evangelistic church is a united church. A divided church is rarely evangelistic.
5. Do small groups and Sunday school classes seek to reach lost persons within their groups? Sunday school was once one of the most effective evangelistic tools in the church. Are the groups in your church evangelistic?
6. Is the leadership of the church evangelistic? The congregation will follow and emulate the priorities of the church leadership.
7. Do the sermons regularly communicate the gospel? They may not be evangelistic sermons in the classic sense, but all sermons should point people to Jesus.
8. Are there ministries in the church that encourage members to be involved in evangelistic outreach and lifestyle? You may be surprised to find how many members become evangelistic with a modest amount of training and equipping.
9. Have programs become ends in themselves rather than means to reach people? Perhaps a total ministry and program audit is in order.
10. Is there any process of accountability for members to be more evangelistic? That which is rewarded and expected becomes the priority of the congregation.[122]

Conclusion

Sometimes these problems are isolated within themselves, but more often, they are symptomatic of some deeper issues that the church faces. When a church falls into decline, it begins to neglect the simple things that can help it grow again. Internal conflicts, discouragement, and uncertainty cause the church to look inward. The revitalization pastor recognizes these issues and leads the church to recapture the ingredients that are necessary for growth. These things used to be present in the church but have lost their priority; therefore, part of the solution is to help the church renew its commitment to the Great Commission. A Great Commission mind-set directs the church to turn its focus away from itself and to reinstate those ingredients necessary for the church to grow.

CHAPTER

14

The Change Matrix

T he vast majority of this book has been dedicated to dealing with assessing church health/church growth issues. Some suggestions have been given about resolving certain conflicts and overcoming certain obstacles. In looking at the big picture, however, how does one go about initializing change without tearing up the church? To be honest, I am not sure that any method will guarantee a smooth transition from one phase of church work to another without some conflict arising.

The following methodology will help to make change more palatable and less painful. No one likes change. Age is irrelevant, as is gender. Everyone reacts negatively to change unless he/she is the one initiating it. Even then, when the change takes place, some of those who wanted the change will express an adverse reaction to the very change they initiated. Such is the church.

The Change Matrix[123]

Initiating change represents one of the most difficult tasks, if not *the* most difficult task, pastors face. Whether one desires to instill an evangelistic DNA into a plateaued congregation or just wants to initiate new ministries or programs, change proves difficult, even impossible. No one

likes change. Someone asked, "How many Baptists does it take to change
a light bulb?" "Change? What do you mean change?"

Dan Southerland, in his book *Transitioning*, expresses very clearly
the dilemma of trying to bring about change in the church, no matter
how advantageous it might be. When he became pastor of his church, the
attendance hovered around three hundred. They grew to eight hundred
and then initiated some changes to help the church to increase its ability
to grow. Almost immediately, the church dropped down to an attendance
of five hundred. Southerland points out that the changes did, in fact,
spur greater growth in his church, but the changes took an initial toll.[124]
Although he does not state this fact, I would assume that most of those
who left were part of the original three hundred who did not like the
changes. The dilemma that most of us face is that we cannot afford to
lose one-third of our congregation, nor do we want to lose them. I would
not presume that Southerland intentionally sought to have three hundred
of his congregants leave his church, but those are the facts he presents.

So how do we initiate change in a less painful and more palatable
manner, especially as we seek to exalt Christ? I do not think that any easy
answers exist, nor do I believe that change can happen overnight (an issue
with which most of us wrestle—we want it to happen now!). I can suggest
a reproducible process that is based upon a biblical model for change. A
biblical model is necessary for several reasons: the fear of being purely
pragmatic; a charge by some in the church who see change as worldly;
the need to be directly connected with the spiritual; and the difficulty
of change. Change becomes difficult because it sometimes is viewed as
attacking the family (i.e., church traditions, standing organizations, or
longtime ministries). It also is tough because some changes are unnecessary. Finally, it is difficult because, as pastors, we need to know "which
hills are worth dying on." Quite honestly, we pick fights over issues that
have little to do with Kingdom work. Therefore, one must know how to
create biblical change.

Let me suggest a four-step course of action that takes time to be initiated and implemented. The Matrix means that all four steps work con-
currently, not just consecutively.[125] They must be repeated consistently.
While the Great Commission never changes, the means by which we

fulfill it does change. The Matrix allows for a constant evaluation of these means.

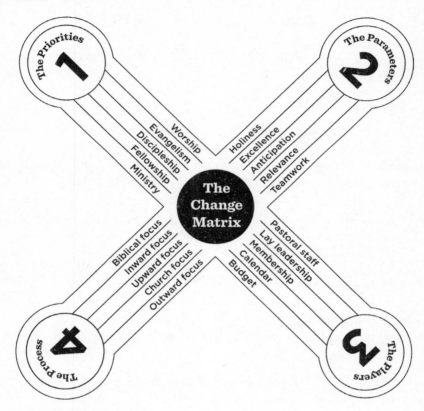

1. The Priorities

First, biblical priorities for the church must be set. Various authors offer suggestions for the priorities of the church,[126] but this particular Matrix utilizes five priorities based upon Acts 2:41–47. In order to communicate these priorities, it is essential that the pastor preach a series of sermons on this topic, along with teaching and repeating these ideas. These standards should also be taught and discussed within the leadership of the church and should lay the foundation for the entire process. The congregation must "buy into" these priorities or the Matrix will not work. Therefore, discussion and discipleship are necessary.

The five priorities include:

1. Worship: Ephesians 5:18–20
2. Evangelism: 2 Corinthians 5:18–19
3. Discipleship: Ephesians 4:11–15
4. Fellowship: 1 John 1:6–7
5. Ministry: 1 Peter 4:7–11

2. The Parameters

An important aspect of helping the church become confident with change develops out of the security of biblical parameters. Many church members find themselves uncomfortable with change because of the fear of pragmatism, so offer the solution by insuring that all change will fall within certain biblical parameters. The pastor must present and not violate this covenant of trust. The remaining two steps (players and process) become the essential means for communicating this trust.

The five parameters include:

1. Holiness: Philippians 3:10; 1 Peter 1:13–21
2. Excellence: Philippians 1:9–11
3. Anticipation: Acts 1:4–5, 14
4. Relevance: 1 Corinthians 9:19–23
5. Teamwork: Philippians 4:1–3

Out of the biblical parameters and priorities, develop a church mission statement and purpose statement. Take time to choose each word carefully, as these statements will define for members and the community the church's vision. See chapter 5 (align all committees and ministries to help the church accomplish its goals) for a more detailed understanding of these two statements.

Here is an example of how that process works. A possible mission statement developed from these parameters and priorities is: Our mission is to *worship* God, to globally *lead* people to faith in Christ, and to *grow* together to be like Him. Once the statement is developed, remind the church of their mission and welcome and invite newcomers to join the fellowship based on this statement. Those three words—*worship, lead,* and *grow*—should serve as the foundation for every ministry, function, and program of the church. Align all ministries so that they accomplish

at least one of these tasks. Use the aforementioned Ministry Fair to promote all three of these ideas. The words should be communicated in the
Discover Class (New Member Class), on all publications, on banners, and
on video screens.

Coupled with this mission statement is a simple purpose statement
that communicates the attitude under which the church operates, such as:
we are a home for your heart with a heart for the world. Repeat often that
statement and use it often as a foundation for ministry and mission. This
process will help the church, and especially newcomers, to catch these
ideas and embrace them.[127]

3. The Players

In order to understand the effectiveness and extent of the change,
communication and evaluation must take place in five specific areas.
These groups provide an essential sounding board that will show the
progress of or resistance to change.

The five players include:

1. Pastoral staff
2. Lay leadership
3. Membership
4. Calendar
5. Budget

In order to communicate the changes necessary, start with the other
pastors or elders of the church. Move then to those in leadership, including church committees, deacons, and Sunday school teachers. Finally, the
need for change must come before the congregation, using whatever form
of church polity is presently in place. Except for very rare occasions, even
if the church follows a pastor-led or elder-led model, the members must
understand the proposed process. One might think that he is leading
the church because he is called the leader, only to discover that no one is
following. Calendar and budget provide important evaluative measures
because the changes are not really implemented until they reflect what
the church does and what it funds.

4. The Process

Finally, a particular process must be followed in order to lead the church to understand the need for change and how these changes will be implemented. The process is truly cyclical, as one must consistently and constantly review the changes made and the future direction of the church. The process also helps the church not to return to a complacency or mediocrity. Even change can become a tradition in itself.

The process includes:

Biblical focus. Be consistent in teaching the church about the centrality of biblical revelation (the truth, inerrancy, and infallibility of Scripture), and make the preaching of the Word primary. Be committed to expository preaching, whereby the depth of the Word is taught and proclaimed. Insist that everything that the church does follows a biblical precedent. Avoid the pragmatism of initiating programs or methods just because they work somewhere else.

Inward focus. The church must be led to discover a "holy dissatisfaction" with their current status or accomplishments. Complacency kills Christians, so they must go through that valley experience whereby they recognize that God has much bigger plans for them. They must answer the questions, "Are we as effective as we can be, and are we accomplishing God's plans for us?"

Upward focus. A key element to finding this "holy dissatisfaction" arises out of a commitment to prayer. Churches pray, but many times those prayers are more vain repetitions than encounters with Christ. As the church leader, lead your church to pray. This prayer focus will move the church to a brokenness about personal sin and will help in leading the church to then re-dream the dream.[128] Being a vision-caster for the church is essential at this moment.[129]

Church focus. Once these new priorities have been set, lead your church to implement the dream. Celebrate with them the victories that the church has and make sure to listen to your people. They will provide a good barometer on the success of the changes made.

Outward focus. In order for believers to see the need for change, they must recognize more fully their role in the Great Commission. As the church leader, help your church to personally get involved in doing missions and ministry outside of the four walls of the church. Partner with organizations that minister to the needs of people. Contact your local association of churches, denomination, church network, parachurch group, or other local churches for help in connecting with missionaries and putting together mission trips. Personally take people on a mission trip![130] Conduct an annual Global Mission Mobilization Celebration.[131]

Conclusion

As the Matrix is implemented, remember that it is a constant, inter-active process, not just a one-time presentation. Continually use it to evaluate the effectiveness of the initiated changes but also employ the practice of accountability. The Matrix offers flexibility for each church to experience God's will and unique vision. Change is never easy, but being wise in bringing about those changes can take away some of the sting and allow for effectiveness through the changes that are put into practice.

Conclusion

W hen wanting to discover what the world thinks about the church, George Barna can serve as an important resource. Not everyone, including myself, always agrees with Barna's solutions, but his research on the twenty-first-century church offers insight into the mind of the unbeliever that the church is trying to reach. Unfortunately, Barna concludes that the church, as a whole, possesses little influence in today's world. He writes, "The seven dominant spheres of influence are movies, music, television, books, the Internet, law, and family. The second tier of influence is comprised of entities such as schools, peers, newspapers, radio, and businesses. The local church appears among entities that have little or no influence on society."[132] Not much affirmation comes from that news.

Ezekiel, Matthew, or Paul could have written the same thing. From the call that God placed on Abraham's life to leave his homeland and travel to the Promised Land to the early beginnings of the church, God's people faced insurmountable obstacles. Sometimes they created their own problems through sin and rebellion. Other times, the hindrances occurred because of human or satanic attack. In every case, God's promises remained true.

Although scores of churches across the world are in need of revitalization, not every pastor is ready for this ministry. To lead a church through revitalization takes risk. It requires time, patience, and a biblical ecclesiology. The rewards, however, remain strong. Jesus promised that He would not give up on the church and neither should we.

When a church begins to decline, many negative attitudes can be encountered, but not everything turns out to be negative in a struggling church. Oftentimes, the decline has led them to a point of desperation. The church is now primed to do something; it just needs the right leader. Dying churches experience a determination that many stable or growing churches do not have. That desperation can be the very motivation needed to turn the church around.

Gary McIntosh tells the story of Thomas Watson, the founder of IBM, who was known for motivational signs that he placed around the office. One such sign simply read: Think. McIntosh interjects:

> One day someone penned the following words under Thomas Watson's think sign: or thwim. While the person who scrawled the extra words was trying to be funny, there is truth in the saying: think or thwim. When it comes to revitalizing a business, or a church, it's sink or swim. There is no possibility of victory in continuing to sink. It is only by swimming toward the future that a church will be revitalized.[133]

So do not ever give up on the church or on a church, for that matter. Even Jesus, though He strongly chided the church in Laodicea, offered this very important invitation, "Listen! I stand at the door and knock. If anyone hears My voice and opens the door, I will come in to him and have dinner with him, and he with Me. The victor: I will give him the right to sit with Me on My throne, just as I also won the victory and sat down with My Father on His throne" (Rev. 3:20–21). If any church has ever existed that was in need of revitalization, the church in Laodicea was it, and yet Jesus did not give up on them.

Not every church will revitalize. Some are destined to die. If Christians are going to stem the tide of decay and loss, they must commit themselves to changing churches around the world. God asked Ezekiel, "Can these bones live?" His response was, "Lord God, only You know." And God does know. So do not give up on the church. Commit to become a revitalization pastor.

Appendix 1

CONNECT WITH US

Date _____   Time of Service_____

Mr/Mrs/Ms _____

Other family in attendance _____

_____

_____

Address _____

City _____

State _____   Zip _____

Phone (H) _____

Phone (C) _____

Email: _____

❏ First-time guest

❏ I'm just visiting

❏ I'm active in another church

❏ Returning guest

❏ I'm looking for a church home

❏ Please mail church information to me

❏ Call me to schedule a visit in my home

How I heard about this church _____

_____

I came as a guest of _____

I am ❏ single   ❏ married
     ❏ widowed   ❏ divorced

Age groups in my home (check all that apply)

❏ Infant - Preschool   ❏ K - 5th grade

❏ 6th - 8th grade   ❏ 9th - 12th grade

❏ College   ❏ Ages 20 - 29

❏ Ages 30 - 39   ❏ Ages 40 - 49

❏ Ages 50 - 59   ❏ Ages 60 - 69

❏ Ages 70 - 79   ❏ Ages 80^{+}

Appendix 2

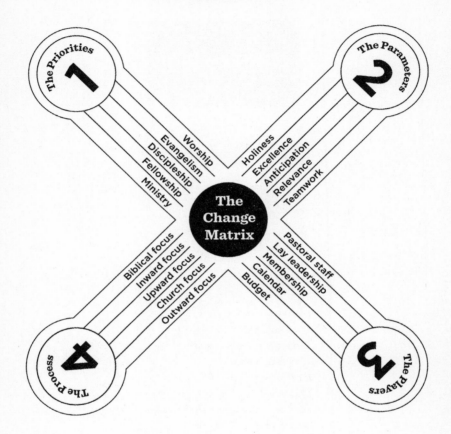

The Priorities 1

Worship
Evangelism
Discipleship
Fellowship
Ministry

The Parameters 2

Holiness
Excellence
Anticipation
Relevance
Teamwork

The Change Matrix

Biblical focus
Inward focus
Upward focus
Church focus
Outward focus

Pastoral staff
Lay leadership
Membership
Calendar
Budget

The Process 4

The Players 3

Appendix 3

 **GREAT COMMISSION MOBILIZATION**

MORNING WORSHIP - 10:45 AM

Kevin Ezell, President of the North American Mission Board, will be challenging our church to be active in mission support.

MISSIONS PREVIEW - 5:00 - 6:00 PM

We will showcase the 2014 opportunities to go "on mission" in Lexington, Georgetown, the U.S., and the World. You will hear from some of our mission partners about their work and needs. Even if you aren't led to "Go," we want to encourage you to attend and be informed of the various ways you can support missions at Porter & NorthPointe through financial support and prayer.

MISSIONS EXHIBIT/FELLOWSHIP - 6:00 - 7:30 PM

Everyone will have the opportunity to meet our church mission partners, learn more about upcoming ministry opportunities, sign up for the 2014 trips, and enjoy food and fellowship.

CHILDREN'S MISSION PARTY - 5:00 - 7:30 PM

This event is being planned for children in grades K-5 in conjunction with Porter's Great Commission Mobilization '14. Kids will be learning about missions in Madagascar as well as other Porter missions partnerships.

Among the other activities planned in the Fellowship Hall will be the showing of the movie, "Madagascar," food, prize giveaways, games, etc. Childcare will be provided for preschoolers ages Birth - 5 yrs. (Pre-K).

Appendix 4

CALVARY CHURCH
DEACON~YOKEFELLOW~PASTOR
COVENANT

1. We will be examples of Christ-like living. We will strive to live exemplary lives, morally, ethically, and spiritually.

2. We will seek to find where God is working and join Him there. His purpose is more important than our pride or program.

3. Everything we do will be undergirded with prayer and done in love for God and for our brothers and sisters in Christ.

4. We will step out in faith believing God can do anything and everything He wills.

5. Our criteria for every decision will be "are we following God's word, Christ's example, and the Holy Spirit's leading?"

6. We will work long and hard with the assumption that ministry is more important than meeting. We will, however, strive to attend every worship service and deacon activity, unless providentially hindered.

7. We will be models of biblical financial stewardship, including tithing.

8. The Pastor and staff will be encouraged to lead with our trust, support, and prayers.

9. Problems will be dealt with and not ignored. Deacons are to be peacemakers bringing reconciliation and grace to any issues and promoting the unity of the body of Christ and the mission of His church.

Appendix 5

Our Core Values

All of our ministries at The Austin Stone have been arranged around these four elements of redemptive life. We live out these values personally, locally, and globally for the glory of God and edification of the church.

Our strategy for ministry is to build up New Testament believers who:

WORSHIP CHRIST

Above all else, we at The Austin Stone are about Jesus. Everyone worships something. We worship what we treasure, what we value most. As believers, we worship Christ because He is the only One truly worthy of such a high level of devotion and affection. "*. . . In Him, the fullness of God dwells in bodily form*" (Colossians 2:9).

Worshipping Christ is the cornerstone of our church. If God is calling you to come on mission with us, He's calling you first and foremost to be a worshipper of Christ.

LIVE IN COMMUNITY

Living in community is the biblical model we see throughout Scripture, first in the Trinity and then in the New Testament Church. Living in Community for the glory of God is one of our best arguments for Jesus among our unbelieving friends and family.

God created us to live in community, and we most effectively live out our mission as the family of God, together.

GET TRAINED

We believe that every saint (believer) is called to be a minister of the gospel, and so every saint must pursue training and discipline to be an effective minister. It is the call of every believer to participate in God's work through the church.

We value getting trained for ministry so that we can put what we know about Him into practice for the building up and edification of the church.

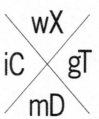

MAKE DISCIPLES

To make disciples literally means "to make learners." We see what it means to make disciples from The Great Commission in Matthew 28:18–20 and in Acts 1:8. We must live on mission personally, locally, and globally, to make much of Christ and bring Him glory.

We believe Christ deserves worship from everyone on earth, and as long as there are people not yet worshipping Him, we still have work to do. It is our desire to complete the task that God has given the church, to preach the gospel to all nations, and hasten the return of Christ! We are all called to make disciples, wherever we are.

Appendix 6

Church Revitalization
Assessment Tool

Finance

- What is the average giving percentage of individuals?
- What is the average giving percentage per family unit?
- What is the per capita weekly giving average in the
    ‣ Previous year?
    ‣ Last three years?
    ‣ Last five years?
- How much debt does the church have?
- How does the church manage its finances and communicate that process to the congregation?
- Is there any system of endowment or legacy giving in place?

Planning/Goal Setting

- Does the church have any kind of planning in place
    ‣ To help the church know where it is going?
    ‣ To help leaders develop a vision?
    ‣ To better allocate resources?
    ‣ To build teamwork?
- What is the church's perspective on
    ‣ Its mission?
    ‣ Its purpose?
    ‣ Its vision?
    ‣ Its plan?
- Where is the church in its vision cycle?
- Does the church have a mission/vision statement, and how does it fit into the mission and purpose of the church?

Growth Barriers

- Who are the Stakeholders (people with a vested interest)?
    ‣ Who are the Stakeholders in the church?
    ‣ Who are the Stakeholders outside the church?
    ‣ What are the Spiritual barriers – the Spiritual Stakeholders?

Growth Barriers (cont'd)

- What are the other barriers the church faces?
  - ‣ Is there a financial recession?
  - ‣ Is there a declining population base?
  - ‣ Is there competition with other churches?
  - ‣ Is the community highly resistant to the gospel?
  - ‣ Is the community stable?

Structures in the Church

- What fellowship structures and opportunities are there in the church?
- What ministry structures and opportunities are there in the church?
- What leadership/governance structures are there in the church?
  - ‣ What structure is currently in place?
  - ‣ What improvements could be made to this structure?
  - ‣ What hindrances are present that will prevent revitalization and growth?
  - ‣ Will the church/denomination be open to allowing any changes in leadership structure?
  - ‣ What hindrances to church revitalization are present because of the current leadership structures?
  - ‣ Are there any ways to work within the system, while at the same time, prevent the hindrances from affecting the church?
- What organizational structures are there in the church?

Outreach/Evangelistic Approaches

- Are members more concerned about the lost than their own preferences and comfort?
- Is the church led to pray for lost persons?
- Are the members of the church open to reaching people who don't look or act like them?
- Do conflicts and critics zap the evangelistic energy of the church?
- Do small groups and Sunday school classes seek to reach lost persons within their groups?
- Is the leadership of the church evangelistic?
- Do the sermons regularly communicate the Gospel?
- Are there ministries in the church that encourage members to be involved in evangelistic outreach and lifestyle?
- Have programs become ends in themselves rather than means to reach people?
- Is there any process of accountability for members to be more evangelistic?

Community Analysis

- How well does the church look like the community?
- How well does the church serve as an advocate for the community?
- Does the church have any healthy partnerships with other churches?

Mission/Vision

- How much is the church driven by mission rather than programming?
- Does the church have its own identity?
- Does the church know God's specific plan for it at this time?

Assimilation Effectiveness

- Does a new person in the church
  - Identify with the goals of the church?
  - Attend worship and special services regularly? (Hebrews 10:25)
  - Attend Communion and Sunday School regularly and have Bible reading and family devotions in the home? (Acts 2:42)
  - Attend some special functions of the congregation such as council meetings, church picnics, special workshops, and midweek services?
  - Grow spiritually? (2 Peter 3:18)
  - Become affiliated with the congregation?
  - Have six or more friends in the church?
  - Have a task or role that is appropriate for his or her spiritual gift(s)? Romans 12; 1 Corinthians 12; Ephesians 4; 1 Peter 4:10-11
  - Become involved in a fellowship group? (Acts 2:42)
  - Give regularly and generously? (1 Corinthians 16:2)
  - Tell others about the Lord and His church? (Matthew 28:18-20; Acts 1:8)

- Does the church as a whole
  - Attract guests and is there a culture to do so?
    - Preach about and pray for new people to come to the church?
    - Provide opportunities for church members to invite their friends?
    - Have a user-friendly Website?
  - Conduct follow-up with first-time guests?
    - How does the church begin follow-up the moment a person steps onto the church campus?
    - Has the church established intentional touches that minister to newcomers and communicate effectively the church's mission?
  - Provide connection points for new people?
    - Does the church have a New Member/Church Information Class?
    - What kind of small group ministry does the church have?
    - What kind of service opportunities for both guests and members does the church provide?

Perceptions/Attitudes

- What is the primary thought of the church about itself?
- What is the primary perspective held by the community about the church?

Data and Statistical Analysis

- What is the worship attendance over the past five years?
- What is the small group Bible study attendance over the past five years?
- What are the budget receipts and expenditures over the past five years?
- What other statistical information is there that would help?

Demographic Assessment

- The church rolls
  - Where do the church members live?
  - What is the age of the membership?
  - What are the marital statuses of the congregation?
  - What is the median income of the congregation?
  - What is the educational level of the congregation?
- The church demographics
  - How many small groups does the church have, where do they meet, and what is their purpose?
  - How many new people have visited the church over the last year to two years?
- The community demographics
  - What are the population changes over the past 5 years and within a 5-mile radius of the church?
  - What are the changes in the housing within a 5-mile radius of the church?

Small Group/Sunday School

- Is there adequate space for present and future growth?
- Do class sizes match room sizes?
- What is the quality of the educational facilities?
- Are new units being created?
- What is the quality of teaching and how much time is allocated for teaching?
- What type of curriculum strategy is in place?
- How is the small group organized?
  - Does each class have a teacher and assistant teacher?
  - Is there a fellowship leader?
  - Is there a process for ministry within and outside the class?
  - Are records kept and does the class follow up with members?

Small Group/Sunday School (cont'd)

- ▸ Is there an outreach/evangelism leader?
- ▸ Is there a prayer leader?
- How does the staff relate to the Sunday school?
  - ▸ Is it a priority of the pastor?
  - ▸ Does the staff have responsibilities within the Sunday school?
  - ▸ Does the staff attend Sunday school?
  - ▸ How often and how well are volunteers recognized and rewarded?
- How does the Sunday school secure new teachers and do teacher training?
- What lines of accountability are in place?

Worship Issues

- What is the primary worship style?
- What worship wars has the church experienced or is the church experiencing?
- How well does the church actually worship?
- What is (are) the primary emphasis of the worship experience?

Prayer Emphasis

- How well does the staff pray together?
- What prayer opportunities are offered to the church?

Missions

- Does the church have a mission plan and vision in place?
- How well does the church see itself as a Great Commission Church?
- Does the church follow through with an Acts 1:8 strategy?

Facilities Analysis

- What is the overall condition of the church property?
- What is the condition of the nursery and children's areas?
- What do the major hallways communicate?
- What does the primary church sign communicate?
- How visible is the church property?
- What is the condition of the most frequently used women's restroom?

Facilities Analysis (cont'd)

- What is the condition of the worship center?
- Where is the main entrance, is it visible, and is there adequate signage?
- How visible is the directional church signage?
- How accessible and available is church parking?

Theological Issues

- Where does the church see itself theologically?
- How does its theology affect its practice?
- Is the church divided over theology?

Ministry–Staff Alignment

- Initial questions to consider
  - Would the church be open to looking for God-called individuals to come in a bi-vocational capacity to help fill the voids?
  - What are the demographics of the church and what do these demographics necessitate regarding staffing?
  - What demographic group will provide the greatest potential for outreach?
- The characteristics of a high-performance team
  - Is there a clear, common purpose?
  - Are there crystal clear roles?
  - Is there accepted leadership?
  - What are the effective processes in place for accomplishing goals?
  - Are there solid, interpersonal relationships?
  - How well does the team communicate?
  - Is there a regular process in place for evaluating staff and staff goals?

Leadership

- The Pastor
  - Am I the right person to lead this church?
  - Can I make the cultural adjustment to this congregation and community?
  - Could I be a more effective leader in another church context?
  - What type of church should I be leading?

Leadership (cont'd)

- The Staff
  - ▸ Who should be on the staff?
  - ▸ What positon should that person hold?
  - ▸ Who does not need to be on the staff?
  - ▸ What is the calling of this person?
  - ▸ Who will be affected by this person's change in position or departure?
  - ▸ What is gained or lost in making this decision?

Appendix 7

Evaluation of Our Mission Statement

	VERY LOW	LOW	AVERAGE	HIGH	VERY HIGH
CLEAR— *Characterized by single-minded direction*	☐	☐	☐	☐	☐
RELEVANT— *Characterized by deep-seated desire*	☐	☐	☐	☐	☐
SIGNIFICANT— *The results to the company if achieved as well as the benefits to me are such that the possibility of success creates enthusiasm, initiative, and energy*	☐	☐	☐	☐	☐
BELIEVABLE— *I believe this task/goal is achievable and will pursue it with bulldog tenacity*	☐	☐	☐	☐	☐
URGENT— *There is a clear time-value attached to the achievement of this mission*	☐	☐	☐	☐	☐
OVERALL MOTIVATION— *Inspires my dedication and commitment*	☐	☐	☐	☐	☐

Notes

1. See Lamar Eugene Cooper Sr., *Ezekiel*, vol. 17, The New American Commentary, ed. Ray Clendenen (Nashville: B&H, 1994), 319–21, for an excellent argument as to the various schools of thought regarding the purpose and theological focus of Ezekiel 37.

2. Stuart Douglas, *Ezekiel*, vol. 20, The Preacher's Commentary Series, ed. John Lloyd Ogilvie (Nashville: Thomas Nelson, 1989), 335.

3. Ed Stetzer and Mike Dodson, *Comeback Churches: How 300 Churches Turned Around and Yours Can Too* (Nashville: B&H, 2007), 19.

4. Thom Rainer, "Autopsy of a Deceased Church," available at http://thom rainer.com/2013/04/24/autopsy-of-a-deceased-church-11-things-i-learned/. Rainer has also put these ideas into book form. See Thom S. Rainer, *Autopsy of a Deceased Church: 12 Ways to Keep Your Church Alive* (Nashville: B&H, 2014).

5. Shawna L. Anderson, Jessica Hamar Martinez, Catherine Hoegeman, Gary Adler, and Mark Chaves, "Dearly Departed: How Often Do Congregations Close?" in the *Journal for the Scientific Study of Religion*, 2008, vol. 47, issue 2, 321–28.

6. Hartford Institute for Religion Research, "Fast Facts about American Religion," http://hirr.hartsem.edu/research/fastfacts/fast_facts.html.

7. Ed Stetzer, "CP Study Part 2: How Many Church Plants Really Survive— And Why?" http://www.namb.net/namb1cb2col.aspx?id=8590001104.

8. Craig L. Blomberg, *Matthew*, vol. 22, The New American Commentary (Nashville: B&H, 1992), 263.

9. John MacArthur, *Slave: The Hidden Truth About Your Identity in Christ* (Nashville: Thomas Nelson, 2010), 15–22, emphasis original.

10. Peter T. O'Brien, *The Epistle to the Philippians: A Commentary on the Greek Text*, The New International Greek Testament Commentary (Grand Rapids: Eerdmans, 1991), 207.

11. Andy McAdams, "The Condition of the Church in America," http://wmson.wordpress.com/2005/12/19/the-condition-of-the-church-in-america/. McAdams serves with a ministry entitled Church Dynamics International. He compiled these statistics.

12. John Kotter and Holger Rathgeber, *Our Iceberg Is Melting: Changing and Succeeding Under Any Conditions* (New York: St. Martin's Press, 2005), 29.

13. John Maxwell, *The 21 Irrefutable Laws of Leadership: Follow Them and People will Follow You* (Nashville: Thomas Nelson, 2007).

14. A good resource for this type of ministry would be Ed Stetzer and Mike Dodson, *Comeback Churches* (Nashville: B&H, 2007). Stetzer and Dodson outline 300 churches with established pastors who led their congregations through revitalization.

15. Tom Cheney, "Does the Church Desire to Grow?" http://www.planter dude.com/media/200.pdf.

16. Carl F. George and Robert E. Logan, *Leading and Managing Your Church: Effective Management for the Christian Professional* (Grand Rapids: Revell, 1987), 147–64.

17. George Gallup Jr., *The Next American Spirituality: Finding God in the Twenty-first Century* (Colorado Springs: Cook Communications, 2002), 163.

18. Thom Rainer, *Surprising Insights from the Unchurched* (Grand Rapids: Zondervan, 2001), 21.

19. George and Logan, *Leading and Managing Your Church*, 161–64.

20. Thom Schultz and Joani Schultz, *Why Nobody Wants to Go to Church Anymore* (Loveland, CO: Group Publishing, 2013), 12–13.

21. Gary L. McIntosh, *There's Hope for Your Church: First Steps to Restoring Health and Growth* (Grand Rapids: Baker Books, 2012), 103–4.

22. Kenneth A. Mathews, *Genesis 11:27–50:26*, vol. 1B, The New American Commentary (Nashville: B&H, 2005), 101–2.

23. John Piper, "Preaching as Worship: Meditations on Expository Preaching," http://www.beginningwithmoses.org/bigger/preacherpiper.htm.

24. See chapter 5 for more information regarding servant evangelism ideas.

25. Geoff Surratt, "3 Not-So-Obvious Reasons Visitors DON'T Return to Your Church," http://www.churchleaders.com/outreach-missions/outreach-missions-articles/171463-geoff-surratt-obvious-reasons-visitors-dont-return-to-your-church.html?utm_source=newsletter&utm_medium=email&utm_campaign=clnewsletter&utm_content=CL+Daily+20131125.

26. John C. Maxwell, *The 5 Levels of Leadership: Proven Steps to Maximize Your Potential* (New York: Center Street, 2011), 2.

27. Ibid., 1.

28. See John 15:1–8, specifically 15:1–2, and 5.

29. John MacArthur, *Ephesians*, The MacArthur New Testament Commentary (Chicago: Moody, 1986), 156.

30. Geoff Surratt, "Why Leadership Training Doesn't Work," http://www.churchleaders.com/outreach-missions/outreach-missions-articles/161305-Why-Leadership-Training-Doesn%E2%80%99t-Work.html?p=3.

31. Ibid.

32. Stetzer and Dodson, *Comeback Churches*, 210–11.

33. Herb Miller, *How to Build a Magnetic Church* (Nashville: Abingdon, 1987), 1.

34. Stetzer and Dodson, *Comeback Churches*, 25–26.

35. Ron Jenson and Jim Stevens, *Dynamics of Church Growth* (Grand Rapids: Baker, 1981), 138.

36. Ibid., 139.

37. Elmer Towns, *10 of Today's Most Innovative Churches* (Ventura, CA: Regal, 1990), 228.

38. Joel D. Heck, *New Member Assimilation* (St. Louis: Concordia, 1988), 54–55.

39. W. E. Vines, *Vine's Expository Dictionary of New Testament Words: A Comprehensive Dictionary of the Original Greek Words with Their Precise Meanings for English Readers* (McLean, VA: MacDonald Publishing, 1968), 575.

40. Steve Sjogren, *101 Ways to Reach Your Community* (Colorado Springs: NavPress, 2000).

41. Timothy K. Beougher, *Overcoming Walls to Witnessing* (Charlotte: Billy Graham Evangelistic Association, 1993).

42. Nelson Searcy, *Ignite: How to Spark Immediate Growth in Your Church* (Grand Rapids: Baker, 2009).

43. Carol Kinsey Goman, "Seven Seconds to Make a First Impression," http://www.forbes.com/sites/carolkinseygoman/2011/02/13/seven-seconds-to-make-a-first-impression/.

44. John Calvin, *Commentary on the Epistle of Paul the Apostle to the Romans*, trans. John Owen (Bellingham, WA: Logos Bible Software, 2010), 335, emphasis original.

45. Charles Arn, "How to Assimilate Newcomers Into Your Church," ChurchGrowth.net, www.churchgrowth.net/seminars/WTF-N1.ppt, n.d. Accessed July 13, 2016.

46. A sample registration tab is included in appendix 1.

47. Chuck Lawless, *Membership Matters: Insights from Effective Churches on New Member Classes and Assimilation* (Grand Rapids: Zondervan, 2005), 54–55.

48. For example, *Uniquely You* offers versatility and allows for an actual scoring for people to discover their gifting.

49. The term Calvary Church is used throughout the book fictitiously to avoid overemphasizing the work or ministry of one particular church.

50. For additional help in developing a mission statement, see appendix 2 and Pat MacMillan, *The Performance Factor* (Nashville: B&H, 2001), 41–60.

51. Thom S. Rainer and Eric Geiger, *Simple Church: Returning to God's Process for Making Disciples* (Nashville: B&H, 2006), 109–226.

52. Colin Marshall and Tony Payne, *The Trellis and the Vine: The Ministry Mind-Shift That Changes Everything* (Kingsford, Australia: Matthias Media, 2009), 17–25.

53. J. P. Lange, P. Schaff, O. Schmoller, and T. W. Chambers, *A Commentary on the Holy Scriptures: Amos* (Bellingham, WA: Logos Bible Software), 24.

54. John S. Hammett and Benjamin L. Merkle, *Those Who Must Give an Account: A Study of Church Membership and Church Discipline* (Nashville: B&H Academic, 2012).

55. Jonathan Leeman and Michael Horton, *Church Membership: How the World Knows Who Represents Jesus* (Wheaton, IL: Crossway, 2012).

56. For further reading on the Ephesian church, see Harold W. Hoehner, *Ephesians: An Exegetical Commentary* (Grand Rapids: Baker, 2002), and Thomas D. Lea and Hayne P. Griffin Jr., *1, 2 Timothy*, vol. 34, The New American Commentary (Nashville: B&H, 1992).

57. Alexander Roberts and James Donaldson, ed., *The Apostolic Father, Justin Martyr, Irenaeus*, vol. 1 in *Anti-Nicene Fathers: The Writing of the Fathers Down to A.D. 325* (Peabody, MA: Hendrickson, 1999), 416.

58. Curtis Vaughn, *1, 2, 3 John*, Study Guide Commentary (Grand Rapids: Zondervan, 1970), 7.

59. John MacArthur, *The MacArthur Study Bible* (Nashville: Word, 1997), 1994.

60. Ideas for these questions came from Rick Warren, "Before You Lead Your Church Through Change," http://pastors.com/before-you-lead-your-church-through-change/.

61. Jim Collins, *Good to Great: Why Some Companies Make the Leap . . . and Others Don't* (New York: Harper Business, 2001), 20–21.

62. Ibid., 47.

63. Pat MacMillan, *The Performance Factor: Unlocking the Secrets of Teamwork* (Nashville: B&H, 2001), 17.

64. Ibid.

65. Ibid., 313–18, emphasis original.

66. Kotter and Rathgeber, *Our Iceberg Is Melting*, 29.

67. See "Demographic Services," http://www.leavellcenter.com/.

68. Dale E. Jones, Sherri Doty, Clifford Grammich, James E. Horsch, Richard Houseal, Mac Lynn, John P. Marcum, Kenneth M. Sanchagrin, and

Richard H. Taylor, *Religious Congregations and Membership in the United States 2000* (Nashville: Glenmary Research Center, 2002).

69. Kotter and Rathgeber, *Our Iceberg Is Melting,* 130–31.

70. D. E. Aune, *Revelation 1–5,* vol. 52a, The Word Biblical Commentary (Dallas: Word, 1998), 218.

71. G. K. Beale, *The Book of Revelation: A Commentary on the Greek Text,* The New International Greek Testament Commentary (Grand Rapids: Eerdmans, 1999), 272–73.

72. James Leo Garrett Jr., *Systematic Theology: Biblical, Historical, and Evangelical,* vol. 2, 2nd ed. (North Richland Hills, TX: BIBAL Press, 2001), 318.

73. Morris Ashcraft, *The Forgiveness of Sins* (Nashville: Broadman Press, 1972), 16–18.

74. Garrett, *Systematic Theology,* vol. 2, 319.

75. Ashcraft, *The Forgiveness of Sins,* 18.

76. J. K. Grider, "Forgiveness," in *Evangelical Dictionary of Theology,* ed. Walter A. Elwell (Grand Rapids: Baker, 1984), 421.

77. Curtis Vaughn, *1, 2, 3 John,* A Bible Study Commentary (Grand Rapids: Zondervan, 1970), 34.

78. Ibid.

79. Herbert Lockyer, *All the Promises of the Bible: A Unique Compilation and Exposition of Divine Promises in Scripture* (Grand Rapids: Zondervan, 1962), 10.

80. Vaughn, *1, 2, 3 John,* 35.

81. Daniel L. Akin, *1, 2, 3 John,* vol. 38, The New American Commentary (Nashville: B&H, 2001), 75.

82. For a more extensive treatment of the Day of Atonement, see William Klassen, *The Forgiving Community* (Philadelphia: Westminster Press, 1966), 79–83.

83. Gerhard Kittel, ed., *Theological Dictionary of the New Testament,* vol. 3 (Grand Rapids: Eerdmans, 1965), 413–31.

84. Michael Bordo and Joseph G. Haubrich, "Deep Recession, Fast Recoveries, and Financial Crises: Evidence from the American Record," www.princeton.edu/jrc/events_archive/repository/second-conference/pdfs/BordoHaubrich22Feb2013withtablesandcharts.pdf.

85. David Platt, *Radical: Taking Back Your Faith from the American Dream* (Colorado Springs: Multnomah, 2010).

86. David Platt, *Radical Together: Unleashing the People of God for the Purpose of God* (Colorado Springs: Multnomah, 2011).

87. Harry L. Reeder III, *From Embers to a Flame: How God Can Revitalize Your Church* (Phillipsburg, NJ: P&R Publishers, 2004), 9.

88. Thom S. Rainer, *The Unchurched Next Door: Understanding Faith Stages as Keys to Sharing Your Faith* (Grand Rapids: Zondervan, 2003), 21–23.

89. Ibid., 261.

90. Barry A. Kosmin and Ariela Keysar, "American Religious Identification Survey (ARIS 2008)," http://b27.cc.trincoll.edu/weblogs/AmericanReligionSurvey-ARIS/reports/ARIS_Report_2008.pdf, 3–7.

91. Ibid., 12.

92. Rainer, *The Unchurched Next Door*, 262.

93. Ibid., 232.

94. Ibid., 266.

95. Ibid., 95–96.

96. Kenneth D. Boa and Robert M. Bowman Jr., *Faith Has Its Reasons: An Integrative Approach to Defending Christianity* (Colorado Springs: NavPress, 2001), 19.

97. Burt Nanus, *Visionary Leadership* (San Francisco: Jossey-Bass, 1992), 3.

98. Hans Finzel, *Change Is Like a Slinky* (Chicago: Northfield Publishing, 2004), 88.

99. Jenson and Stephens, *Dynamics of Church Growth*, 50–51.

100. Aubrey Malphurs, *Developing Vision for Ministry in the 21st Century* (Grand Rapids: Baker, 1999), 30–31.

101. Ibid., 32.

102. Ibid., 32–40.

103. Robert D. Dale, *To Dream Again: How to Help Your Church Come Alive* (Eugene, OR: Wipf and Stock, 1981), 5.

104. Ibid., 35–123.

105. Malphurs, *Developing a Vision for Ministry*, 187.

106. Will Mancini, "Vision and Strategy Church Trends for 2011 and Beyond," http://www.willmancini.com/2011/01/vision-and-strategy-church-trends-for-2011-and-beyond.html.

107. Brian Orme, "A Candid Talk with Francis Chan on Evangelism and Mission," http://www.outreachmagazine.com/people/4922-francis-chan-why-the-church-is-weak-at-evangelism.html.

108. Anthony Casurella, "Fellowship," in *Dictionary of the Later New Testament and its Development*, Ralph P. Martin and Peter H. Davids, eds. (Downers Grove, IL: InterVarsity, 1997), 373.

109. Lawless, *Membership Matters*, 49.

110. Shaye J. D. Cohen, *From the Maccabees to the Mishnah* (Louisville: John Knox Press, 2006), 101–3.

111. Obviously, churches are structured differently, some with deacons, others with elders, and still others with both groups. Depending on church polity, these groups may function differently with varying degrees of authority. The key issue is to move beyond the power struggles and find ways to influence those who influence the church. The next sections of this chapter will elaborate on this matter.

112. See appendix 4.

113. John Piper, *Brothers, We Are Not Professionals: A Plea to Pastors for Radical Ministry* (Nashville: B&H, 2002), 11, emphasis original.

114. Jonathan Edwards, "The End for Which God Created the World," in vol. 1 of *The Works of Jonathan Edwards* (Peabody, MA: Hendrickson, 2003), 105.

115. Chip Turner, "Control Issues Head List for Pastoral Terminations," http://www.sbclife.net/Articles/2012/10/sla7.asp.

116. Robert Naylor, *The Baptist Deacon* (Nashville: Broadman Press, 1955), 3.

117. H. Richard Niebuhr, *The Purpose of the Church and Its Ministry: Reflections on the Aims of Theological Education* (New York: Harper & Brothers, 1956), 69.

118. Jim Nicodem, "7 Ways to Get Your Church Onto the Praying Field," http://www.churchleaders.com/pastors/pastor-how-to/138200-7-ways-to-get-your-church-onto-the-praying-field.html.

119. Jenson and Stevens, *Dynamics of Church Growth*, 26.

120. Rick Ezell, "5 Must-Know Facts About First-Time Guests," http://www.churchleaders.com/pastors/pastor-articles/153325-5-important-facts-about-first-time-guests.html?p=1.

121. Ibid.

122. Thom S. Rainer, "10 Questions to Diagnose the Evangelistic Health of Your Church," http://www.christianpost.com/news/10-questions-to-diagnose-the-evangelistic-health-of-your-church-80583/.

123. The initial idea of the Change Matrix was developed with the help of Adam W. Greenway, Dean of the Billy Graham School of Missions, Evangelism, and Ministry at The Southern Baptist Theological Seminary.

124. Dan Southerland, *Transitioning: Leading Your Church Through Change* (Grand Rapids: Zondervan, 1999), 127.

125. See appendix 2.

126. See Rick Warren, *The Purpose-Driven Church: Growth Without Compromising Your Method and Mission* (Grand Rapids: Zondervan, 1999); Gene Mims, *Kingdom Principles for Church Growth* (Nashville: LifeWay Press, 2004); Chuck Lawless, *Discipled Warriors: Growing Healthy Churches That Are Equipped for Spiritual Warfare* (Grand Rapids: Kregel, 2002).

127. The use of biblical priorities and parameters can also be structured in what many churches call their core values. An example of these core values is included in appendix 5 from the Austin Stone Community Church in Texas. It is used by permission.

128. An excellent study at this point is Claude King, *Come to the Lord's Table: A 28-Day Devotional Guide* (Nashville: LifeWay Press, 2006). This study is intended for making preparation for the Lord's Supper, but it is much more

than that. It will lead people through a time of personal repentance, biblical obedience, and the restoration of broken relationships. It can be a powerful tool for helping the church develop an upward focus.

129. See Robert Dale, *To Dream Again*.

130. For additional help, see William D. Henard, "The Great Commission Leader: The Pastor as Personal Evangelist," in *Great Commission Resurgence: Fulfilling God's Mandate in Our Time*, ed. Chuck Lawless and Adam W. Greenway (Nashville: B&H Academic, 2010), 265–80, and William D. Henard, "How to Develop a Great Commission Church," in *Mobilizing a Great Commission Church for Harvest: Voices and Views from the Southern Baptist Professors of Evangelism Fellowship*, ed. Tom Johnston (Eugene, OR: Wipf & Stock, 2011), 51–63.

131. See appendix 3.

132. George Barna, *Revolution* (Ventura, CA: Barna Books, 2005), 118.

133. McIntosh, *There's Hope for Your Church*, 168.